AFRICA IN THE MODERN WORLD

Edited by GWENDOLEN M. CARTER
Director, Program of African Studies
Northwestern University

The Cameroon Federal Republic
by Victor T. Le Vine

Ethiopia: The Modernization of Autocracy
by Robert L. Hess

Liberia: The Evolution of Privilege
by J. Gus Liebenow

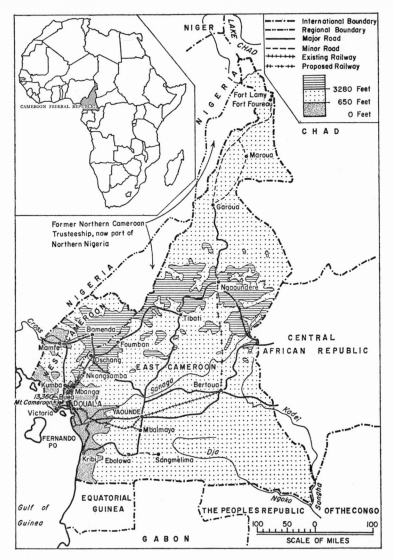

Map 1. The Cameroon Federal Republic

THE CAMEROON
FEDERAL REPUBLIC

VICTOR T. LE VINE

WASHINGTON UNIVERSITY, ST. LOUIS
AND THE UNIVERSITY OF GHANA, LEGON

Cornell University Press

ITHACA AND LONDON

First published 1971 by Cornell University Press.
Published in the United Kingdom
by Cornell University Press Ltd.,
2–4 Brook Street, London W1Y 1AA.

International Standard Book Number 0-8014-0637-4
Library of Congress Catalog Card Number 70-148025

PRINTED IN THE UNITED STATES OF AMERICA
BY VAIL-BALLOU PRESS, INC.

Foreword

This study of the Cameroon Federal Republic provides many insights into the characteristics and development of a country whose history contrasts strikingly with that of many other independent African states. Most remarkable, the Cameroon Federal Republic has functioned as a stable federal system since 1961, whereas both the Mali and the Central African federations broke up in the post-1958 period (the former lasted eighteen months, 1959–1960, the latter from 1953 to 1963). The Ethiopian-Eritrean Federation (1952–1962) was absorbed into the unified Ethiopian Empire, and the Federation of Nigeria (established in 1960) suffered a tragic civil war.

In developing its distinctive federal institutions and ways of making them work, the Cameroon Federal Republic has had to cope with manifold problems. One set of difficulties lies in the great disparity in size between its two units, the relatively small former British Southern Cameroons and the ten-times-larger former French Cameroun. Moreover, as a result of their separate colonial experiences, the two units have evolved very different political cultures, political structures, and forms of economic organization. Following the characteristic pattern of French administration, East Cameroon retains a centralized structure while West Cameroon's characteristically British system of political decentralization is still reflected in its internal organization. Paradoxically, however, the larger unit is characterized by the activities of independent farmers and small businessmen whereas in the former British area, at least in the coastal zone, economic life is dominated by the large-scale Cameroon Development Corporation. Another feature differentiating the two units is that West Cameroon includes a large number of migrants from what was the former Northern Cameroons, that part of the old trust territory incorporated into the Federation of Nigeria by the plebiscite of 1961.

In the stability and consistency of its northern leadership, the Cameroon Federal Republic is similar to its huge neighbor, Nigeria. In both countries, the southern area is far more developed economically than the northern sector but the effect on political life, in both countries, has been to produce great diversity and rivalries. In both Nigeria and Cameroon, the inability of factions to combine into a cohesive partnership in practice has prevented the more advanced southern areas from challenging the political power position of the north. In Cameroon, the astuteness of Ahmadou Ahidjo, its top leader since 1958, has been an additional factor in northern political dominance. Ahidjo, a Fulani from Garoua (in the north), has emphasized the national character of his government, while ensuring that his northern colleagues controlled the most important ministerial and legislative posts.

Although these examples of the greater political solidarity of less economically developed areas are not of themselves conclusive, they bear an interesting parallel to the situation in the United States, and, to a lesser degree, in France. It appears that it is not only in developing countries that economic diversity and expansion tend to fragment political forces and create tensions and instability.

The Cameroon Federal Republic is situated at cultural, linguistic, historical, and geographic crossroads between West and Equatorial Africa. Its closest associations have been within UDEAC (Central African Customs and Economic Union) whose other members are the former French territories of Equatorial Africa—Gabon, Central African Republic, Chad, and Congo (Brazzaville)—and with the loosely associated members of OCAM (Joint African and Malagasy Organization). In these groupings Cameroon stands out by the degree of its independence from France and the extent of its Africanization of key posts in the civil service as well as other fields. This degree of African control in all facets of life is not only noticeable in comparison with the weaker French-speaking states but also with the Ivory Coast, which possesses one of the strongest economies and most stable political systems in Africa. The explanation may be at least in part that the impact of the radical UPC (Union des Populations du Cameroun) led the French government to regard Cameroon as lacking the docility of the Ivory Coast which, under its long-time leader Félix Houphouet-Boigny, has pursued a policy of close association with France since 1951. A by-product of this working together is that the Ivory Coast has retained many more French civil servants in its administration than did the Cameroon, although this situation may result even more from the fact that school enrollments in Cameroon have been proportionately higher and more evenly distributed than in the Ivory Coast.

No one would suggest that the Cameroon Federal Republic is without serious strains and problems. No African-controlled country is without such difficulties. But Cameroon has successfully survived as a functioning federal entity in a period when many apparently more fortunately endowed states have not. It possesses highly experienced leadership, and its top figure is still young (he was forty-six in 1970). Both because of its strategic position within the continent and because of the interest of its institutions and characteristic features, the Cameroon Federal Republic deserves our particular attention.

GWENDOLEN M. CARTER

Northwestern University

Acknowledgments

The field research on which the original version of this study was based would not have been possible without the support of the Ford Foundation, whose Foreign Area Fellowship Program enabled me to spend a year in Cameroon. Grateful acknowledgment is made of that support and of the assistance and valuable counsel provided by Dr. James S. Coleman, former director of the African Studies Center, University of California, Los Angeles.

Two subsequent visits to Cameroon, in May 1965 and April 1971, made it possible to assess further political, social, and economic developments in the country. In addition, and because my visits were of relatively short duration, I have relied on the analyses of scholars whose recent publications deal in depth with matters that I only glimpsed in passing. Those to whom I am most indebted are Willard Johnson, Edwin Ardener, Claude Welch, and Philippe Hugon.

Responsibility for the final product is, of course, mine alone, and I hope that some of my less sanguine judgments may be proved wrong in time.

VICTOR T. LE VINE

University of Ghana, Legon

Contents

Maps

Tables

Abbreviations

ATUC   African Trade Union Confederation. African regional trade-union organization, founded in 1962.

BDC   Bloc Démocratique Camerounais. Catholic-oriented party, 1951–1955; in East Cameroon, precursor to the Parti des Démocrates Camerounais (see PDC).

CCSC   Confédération Camerounaise des Syndicats Croyants. Confessional—mainly Protestant—trade-union federation, East Cameroon.

CDCWU   Cameroon Development Corporation Workers' Union. Important West Cameroon trade union.

CFU   Cameroons Federal Union. Early (1947–1949) West Cameroon political party.

CGCT   Confédération Générale Camerounaise du Travail. East Cameroon trade union.

CNF   Cameroons National Federation. West Cameroon political grouping (1949–1951).

CNU   Cameroon National Union. (Also known by its French name: Union Nationale Camerounaise—UNC.) The single national party in Cameroon since 1966.

CPNC   Cameroon Peoples National Convention. West Cameroon political party (1959–1966).

CUC   Cameroon United Congress. West Cameroon splinter party, 1965–1966.

CYL   Cameroons Youth League. Early (1940–1949) Lagos-based West Cameroon nationalist group.

FPUP   Front Populaire pour l'Unité et la Paix. Parliamentary grouping of Bamiléké deputies, 1960–1961, East Cameroon.

FSC	Fédération des Syndicats du Cameroun. Nonconfessional East Cameroon trade-union federation.
ICFTU	International Confederation of Free Trade Unions. Non-Communist international trade-union organization.
IFCTU	International Federation of Christian Trade Unions. Confessional—mainly Catholic—group of trade unions.
KNC	Kamerun National Congress. West Cameroon political party.
KNDP	Kamerun National Democratic Party. West Cameroon political party, founded in 1955 by John N. Foncha.
KPP	Kamerun Peoples' Party. West Cameroon political party.
MANC	Mouvement d'Action Nationale Camerounaise. Political party in East Cameroon, 1956–1960.
NCNC	National Council of Nigeria and the Cameroons. Nigerian political party to which some early West Cameroon nationalists belonged. (Later renamed National Convention of Nigerian Citizens when Cameroon Federation was formed in 1961.)
OAU	Organization of African Unity.
OCAM	Organisation Commune Africaine et Malagache. International grouping of French-speaking African states, since 1965.
OK	One Kamerun (party). West Cameroon branch of the Union des Populations du Cameroun (see UPC).
PDC	Parti des Démocrates Camerounais. East Cameroon political party led by A. M. Mbida, 1958–1966. (Also known as the DC—Démocrates Camerounais.)
PSC	Parti Socialiste Camerounais. Organized in 1959 by Charles Okala, mainly active in East Cameroon.

PTC   Parti Travailliste Camerounais. Short-lived (1962) East Cameroon political party.

RDA   Rassemblement Démocratique Africain. Transterritorial African political party, founded in 1946.

UC   Union Camerounaise. East Cameroon political party, founded 1958 by Ahmadou Ahidjo.

UCTC   Union Camerounaise des Travailleurs Croyants. Confessional—mainly Catholic—East Cameroon trade-union confederation.

UDEAC   Union Douanière et Economique de l'Afrique Centrale. Also known as the Central African Customs and Economic Union. Customs and economic organization of French-speaking equatorial African states and Cameroon.

UGTAN   Union Générale des Travailleurs d'Afrique Noire. "Radical" interterritorial trade-union organization formed in 1957.

UGTC   Union Générale des Travailleurs du Cameroun. East Cameroon trade union.

UNC   Union Nationale Camerounaise. See CNU.

UPC   Union des Populations du Cameroun. East Cameroon political party founded in 1948; once the most important nationalist group, later (1955–1960) banned. Merged with CNU, 1966.

USAC   Union des Syndicats Autonomes Camerounais. East Cameroon trade union.

USC   Union Sociale Camerounaise. Socialist party in East Cameroon, precursor to PSC (see PSC).

USCC   Union des Syndicats Croyants du Cameroun. East Cameroon trade-union federation. Another trade-union federation with these initials (Union des Syndicats Confédérés du Cameroun) existed in East Cameroon during the 1950's.

USLC   Union des Syndicats Libres du Cameroun. East Cameroon trade-union grouping.

UTC   Union des Travailleurs Camerounais (Workers' Union of Cameroon). "Umbrella" organization of principal West and East Cameroon trade-union federations (see USCC, FSC, and WCTUC).

WCTUC   West Cameroon Trade Union Congress. Groups most of West Cameroon's trade-union organizations.

WFTU   World Federation of Trade Unions. Communist-dominated international trade-union organization.

Introduction

When the original version of this study was written, in 1962, the Cameroon federation was barely a year old. The political ambiguities that surrounded the formation of the new union and the various economic and social difficulties that the young nation inherited suggested a cautious prognosis of the viability of the federation. Today, nearly a decade later, the Federal Republic not only has managed to face up to its problems, but seems well on the way to becoming one of contemporary Africa's more successful political systems. It is impossible, naturally, to predict the course of events in Cameroon with certainty, but it appears that few insuperable problems are likely to cloud Cameroon's immediate future. In 1962 it was easy to underestimate President Ahidjo's leadership. Now much of the credit for the success of the federation must go to him; he must be counted, I think, as one of Africa's most resourceful, intelligent, and pragmatic leaders.

"Complexity" is the key word to describe Cameroon's political, social, and economic configurations. No other African country, save perhaps Nigeria, has had such an extraordinarily varied history of political experiences. It saw three direct colonial and two indirect tutelary powers work their will and influence: Germany, France, and Great Britain; the League of Nations and the United Nations. Nigeria, with which the British Cameroons were in administrative union, might be added to the list. Further, the territory ran the gamut from a multiparty to a single-party system. In an earlier work, I listed no fewer than 117 East Cameroonian political parties and groups active before independence.[1] That figure may be too modest, since several groups I did not list have since come to my attention, and, it does not, of course, include the score or so parties and groups active in the British Cameroons. I have attempted in this book to describe in summary form the process whereby the political parties were gradually reduced to one, but the story is admittedly much more complicated and rich in detail than any brief résumé can suggest. There is, finally, the story of the Union des Populations du Cameroun (UPC), which runs through Cameroon's political history as a dominant theme until the early 1960's, when the organization faded both as an internal political power and as an external irritant to the regime of President Ahidjo. That story I have only summarized in this book because both Willard Johnson and I have dealt extensively with it elsewhere (see the Bibliography). Even our discussions there deal only with the externals, and when the story is finally told in its entirety (perhaps by one of its participants) it must reflect some of the tragedy, frustration, and sheer desperation that befell one of the truly revolutionary movements of contemporary Africa.

Cameroon's political complexities have been, to some extent, the mirror of the country's exceptional social and ethnic diversity. Official sources have claimed that there are more than 136 identifiable ethnic groups in East

---

[1] *The Cameroons from Mandate to Independence* (Berkeley and Los Angeles: University of California Press, 1964), pp. 235–247.

Cameroon and at least 70 such groups in the western state.[2] Exactly how many there are depends, of course, on whose classification you adopt, and this is a matter best left to the ethnographers. The fact remains that Cameroon presents an ethnic and social pluralism of bewildering complexity. It is a picture further complicated (to cite but a few examples) by internal migrations of considerable importance, by the presence of large numbers of Eastern Nigerians in West Cameroon, by the demographic and social dynamism of the Bamiléké, by the comparative backwardness of the northern Kirdi people, and by the continued presence in the north and west of tribal and semi-feudal political structures left over from earlier centuries. No small part of Cameroon's political problems stem from the task of integrating so diverse a set of populations into a single national system. Moreover, superimposed on ethnic diversity is the bilingualism inherited from colonial days, as well as the problems of trying to reconcile political, administrative, educational, and social habits developed over forty years of separate colonial rule.

Cameroon's economy deserves to be analyzed by a professional economist; I have attempted to render in broad outlines what is, again, a most complex subject. The picture presented is that of a country without an exceptional resource base trying to modernize and extend its agricultural sector (on which it depends for most of its foreign exchange), while simultaneously seeking to build up a modest industrial capacity. Cameroon is lucky to have the

[2] *Ibid.,* p. 6. The West Cameroonian figure is derived from a map, "West Cameroon, Tribal Boundaries," issued by the Land and Survey Department, Buea, 1959, drawn from data of Edwin Ardener.

means and the resources to diversify its agriculture so that it will not have to be utterly dependent on coffee and cocoa, its leading crops. But that is still somewhat in the future, albeit a realizably near future. The pages following will make considerable point of the economy's short-comings; and, indeed, they must be noted along with its strong points. What is, however, important to remember at the outset—and I shall come back to this point again—is that it is basically a strong economy, with the resources, the human talent, and (where necessary) the foreign finan-cial friends to make it grow much stronger in the future. Such optimism, is, of course, hedged with the inevitable "ifs": the need to integrate regional, subregional, and even tribally based economic systems into the broader national economy; the imperatives of extending infrastructures to carry such integrative initiatives and the new industries they promote; and finally, the maintenance of a planning apparatus that can set both feasible economic goals and realistic priorities.

A number of different spellings of "Cameroon" are used in this book to identify the components of the present federation at various stages of their political evolution. The spellings are those employed during those periods. "Kamerun" refers to the German protectorate; this spell-ing was sometimes used by nationalists. "Cameroun," the French spelling, was used in what is now East Cameroon during the periods of the French mandate and trusteeship and during the period of the Republic of Cameroun and is still used in the French-speaking East Cameroon. "Cam-eroon" or "Cameroons," the anglicized version, was used to refer to the Cameroons under United Kingdom man-date and later trusteeship and is still used by the English-speaking inhabitants of West Cameroon. "Southern Cameroons" was the southern administrative half of the former Cameroons under British trusteeship, the section which now corresponds to West Cameroon. "Northern Cameroons" was the northern section of the British Cameroons, the part of the former trusteeship which, in February 1961, elected to merge with Nigeria. "Cameroon" in this book will be used to refer *generally* to the territory, to the federation, or to either of its components.

Cameroonian names are not always consistently spelled, even by Cameroonians. Unfortunately, no simple convention exists on spelling or usage, save that the family or clan name must always appear. Two names illustrate the problem: E. Egbe Tabi is also referred to as E. T. Egbe, E. Tabi Egbe, and E. Egbe; A. N. Jua is also known as A. Ngom Jua, A. Jua Ngom, or simply A. Jua. The family names here are Egbe and Jua, and these men are sometimes referred to simply by these names. This problem arises only for southerners with double or hyphenated names, and usually not among northerners or individuals with a single surname.

Even if events, unforeseeable at this moment, alter the picture of contemporary Cameroon, nothing can detract from the friendliness and hospitality of its people, and from the very real sense of accomplishment that all Cameroonians must feel on the eve of their country's tenth anniversary.

THE CAMEROON
FEDERAL REPUBLIC

CHAPTER 1

Historical Background

Cameroon is unique among African states in the remarkable variety of its historical experiences. Once a major
portion of the infamous west African slave coast, it became
a German protectorate; then, divided, it was transformed
into two League of Nations mandates. Thereafter by
further metamorphoses, it became two United Nations
trust territories. Finally, with the passing of the trustee-
ships, there was brief independence for one part, and then
unification of both in an independent federal republic.

Cameroon's experiment in federalism is not without its
unusual aspects. It is thus far the only federal union of
French- and English-speaking territories on the continent
(not excepting the Ghana-Guinea-Mali union, which never
went beyond the rhetorical stage) and the first attempt to
blend the political offspring of French, British, and United
Nations tutelary experiences. Moreover, it also represents
an attempt to provide the two parts of the federation, separated by forty years of administrative, political, and economic development under different colonial regimes, with
a viable formula for coexistence under the same constitutional roof. The only other African bilingual territorial
merger, that of the Somalis, resulted in a unitary state.

Unique too is the fact that Cameroon lies at important
geographical and demographic crossroads; it divides the
Niger and Congo river basins, but shares physical characteristics of both, and it is the ethnic shatter zone where

1

cultures of both regions meet and mingle. Cameroonian political development, then, can be understood only in the light of the interaction between the complex physical and human facts of Cameroon's experience.

The Precolonial Period

There is some question concerning the period in which Cameroon is first noticed by recorded history. According to some interpretations of the celebrated *Periplus* of the Carthaginian Hanno, who claimed to have sailed the coast of the "Lybic lands beyond the Pillars of Hercules," the farthest extent of his voyage is believed to have been the Bight of Biafra, where he and his crews beheld volcanic eruptions of Mount Cameroon and on the island of Fernando Po. However one reads Hanno, there is no question that insofar as recorded European history is concerned, the Portuguese were the first Europeans to reach the Cameroon coast, to visit the island of Fernando Po, and to sail into the estuary of what is now known as the Wouri River, near the site of modern Douala. The year was probably 1472, a date which also marks the occasion on which the Portuguese named the river Rio dos Camaroes, or River of Prawns, after catching and eating—and mistaking for prawns—a variety of crayfish found occasionally in the estuary. The name stuck and subsequently was generally applied to the entire coastal area between Mount Cameroon and Rio Muni (formerly Spanish Guinea).[1]

[1] See Joseph Bouchaud, *La Côte du Cameroun dans l'histoire et la cartographie des origines à l'annexion allemande* (Yaoundé: IFAN, Centre du Cameroun, 1952), and Engelbert Mveng, *Histoire du Cameroun* (Paris: Présence Africaine, 1963), pp. 15–260 for a full discussion of the precolonial period. Fernando Po, Rio Muni, and

The early Portuguese visitors to the Rio dos Camaroes opened the adjacent coastal areas to the slave trade, a commerce that had begun to flourish after 1530, when the burgeoning plantations in the New World found imported African labor increasingly necessary. For the next three centuries the Cameroon coast was systematically exploited for its human commodity, with Portuguese, Spanish, French, British, American, and German traders competing for a share of the market. In the process, the Spanish acquired Fernando Po, using it as one of their main collection points for slaves taken along the Bight of Benin. French, German, and British traders established semipermanent posts along the coast, principally at the mouth of the Wouri, where the indigenous Douala became useful middlemen in the traffic of slaves.

By the beginning of the nineteenth century, European, and particularly British, sentiment had begun to turn against continuation of the slave trade, a development which coincided with the establishment of British predominance in west African waters from Dakar to the Gulf of Guinea. In 1827 Britain obtained permission from the Spanish to occupy Fernando Po for the purpose of basing a squadron to control the shipment of slaves from the Bights of Biafra and Benin. By the 1830's and 1840's, the British had explored the interior for some distance and, under the aegis of one of their itinerant consuls, established a "court of equity" for the multinational trading community at Douala. Finally, in 1858, Alfred Saker, at the head of an English Baptist mission community, established

---

several small nearby islands became the independent Republic of Equatorial Guinea on October 12, 1968.

the first permanent European settlement, Victoria, at the foot of Mount Cameroon.

The extent of British influence along the Cameroon coast, at Douala, and in the Gulf of Guinea, coupled with repeated demands from various Cameroonian chiefdoms for British protection, made annexation of the area by Britain seem a foregone conclusion. This conclusion was not shared by either the French or the Germans. The French established a number of trading posts southward along the coast, signing treaties in the process with a number of local chiefs. German commercial interests, long active in the Cameroon area, had by 1882 convinced Bismarck of the desirability of extending imperial protection to the Cameroon coast. Quietly, and under the unsuspecting nose of the Gladstone government, Bismarck in the spring of 1884 dispatched Gustav Nachtigal—explorer and lately German consul general in Tunis—to the Guinea coast, ostensibly to investigate the "state of German commerce" in the area. In the meantime, a dilatory British government, having finally become aware of the possibility that the Cameroon coast might fall into other, particularly French, hands, authorized their itinerant "floating consul," Edward Hyde Hewett, to conclude treaties of annexation with the petty "kings" at Douala. Hewett, to his eternal chagrin, arrived in Douala a week too late. On July 12, 1884, Nachtigal, who had arrived the day before, signed a treaty with two of the Douala kings establishing the German protectorate.[2]

[2] The circumstances surrounding the German annexation of the Cameroons and the nature of their protectorate over the territory are detailed in Harry Rudin's excellent study, *Germans in the Cameroons* (New Haven: Yale University Press, 1938), and in René

Colonial Rule

THE KAMERUN PROTECTORATE

The German protectorate lasted thirty years. Under a succession of governors of varying abilities, the protectorate was extended by 1911 to the edge of Lake Chad in the north and was almost doubled in size in that year following a deal with France in which substantial chunks of the then French Congo were ceded to Germany in return for the withdrawal of imperial interests in Morocco. Moreover, the German administration laid the foundation for modern Cameroon's social overhead capital (that is, basic transportation, communication, irrigation, and power facilities): wharves and docks at Douala, Kribi, Campo, Tiko, and Victoria; rail lines north from Douala to Nkongsamba and west almost to Yaoundé, as well as the narrow-gauge railroad serving Victoria Plantation; a large number of bridges, roads, and paths; and well-constructed public and private buildings, many of which are still in use today. Furthermore, the plantations and development projects begun by the Germans cannot be overlooked. In all, the French and British inherited in the two Cameroons an established basis for further economic development, that is, a basic infrastructure and a productive plantation economy, both with considerable potential for further growth.

Douala Manga Bell, "Contribution à l'histoire du Cameroun de 1884 à 1914," *L'Effort Camerounais* (Yaoundé), Nos. 210–223 (Oct. 25, 1959–Jan. 24, 1960). See also Mveng, *op. cit.,* pp. 269–294. An East German—and Marxist—version of the protectorate period is provided in Helmuth Stoecker, ed., *Kamerun unter deutscher Kolonialherrschaft* (Berlin: Rütten and Loening, 1960).

The Kamerun protectorate also left behind some less easily measurable legacies. By encouraging missionary and educational activity, the Germans consciously developed an indigenous Cameroonian stratum capable of mediating between Europeans and the Africans of the hinterland. By introducing large numbers of Cameroonians to the money economy, the Germans effectively laid the basis for urban life in the southern portions of the country and for the subsequent growth of an indigenous trading community. The Germans have often, and with some justice, been accused of using harsh methods to further their aims. Objective examination of the facts reveals that whatever can be said of some of their methods or motives, the Germans maintained a colonial administration in the Kamerun that compares favorably with any other in Africa at the time. In another context, however, the quality of German rule becomes irrelevant. Cameroonians of later periods, anxious to attack the French or British administrations for alleged wrongs of commission or omission, found that the brighter the German experience could be painted, the more useful it became as a political weapon. The "Kamerun" became, in this connection, an important touchstone for Cameroonian nationalists, a potent and evocative symbol of a half-mythical "golden age" when the Cameroon was one and undivided.[3]

[3] For elaborations on this theme, see Edwin Ardener, "The Kamerun Idea," *West Africa,* June 7 and 14, 1958, and Victor T. Le Vine, "The Politics of Partition in Africa: The Cameroons and the Myth of Unification," *Journal of International Affairs,* XVII (1964), 198–210.

World War I brought the Kamerun protectorate to an abrupt end. Between 1914 and 1916, French, British, and Belgian troops, invading the Kamerun from several sides, gradually converged upon Yaoundé, the administrative capital, forcing the German forces south and into eventual internment in Spanish Guinea. Upon the departure of the Germans, the British and French created a short-lived condominium over the territory that ended in March 1916, when the victors agreed on a provisional partition of the territory. This *ad hoc* partition divided the country into two unequal parts. The British accepted two noncontiguous portions in the west bordering Nigeria that amounted to about one-fifth of the territory's total area. The French took the remainder, after returning to their Chad colony territories ceded to Kamerun in 1911. The partition was confirmed by the Versailles peace treaties, and in 1922, after some French hesitation (France wanted to convert the territory into a colony), the two Cameroons became League of Nations mandated territories under the respective administrations of France and the United Kingdom. The creation of the mandates marked the beginning of thirty-five years of separate administrative, economic, and political existence for the two Cameroons. It was not until 1947 that the question of reuniting them was again raised.

Except for German agitation in the southern section, life in the British Cameroons mandate was relatively uneventful during the interwar period. The territory, joined to Nigeria in an administrative union, was generally considered somewhat of a backwater to the mainstream of

Nigerian development. The forces which were shaping the course of Nigerian and French Cameroonian events had few echoes in the British Cameroons; both Africans and Europeans in the territory were more concerned with economic than political problems. In general, contacts between the two Cameroons fluctuated according to the tide of labor going from the French to the British mandate and with the scattered commercial relations maintained across the border. Contacts with Nigeria were similarly sparse, including seasonal labor coming in from eastern Nigeria and some commercial links overland with eastern Nigeria and by the way of the Cross River. Miserable roads, and generally poor communications, accentuated the territory's physical isolation.

By far the most important influence on the economic development of the British mandate was the group of German plantations in the British Southern Cameroons, repurchased by most of their former owners after 1924. Within two years after their return, the Germans, who made up the largest European group in the territory, had begun to make their plantations pay. As a consequence of their activity, trade with Germany from 1925 to 1938 was the territory's principal source of revenue. With the rise of Hitler, German settler sentiment became increasingly pro-Nazi and militantly nationalist—to such an extent, in fact, that with the coming of World War II the German community in the British Cameroons might well have been termed a small "fifth column." During the war, however, these Germans were repatriated and their plantations once again expropriated.

Finally, a word must be said about British policies in the Cameroons north of the Southern Cameroons plantation area. Here, indirect rule seems to have worked quite well. With the possible exception of the so-called Kirdi areas (see p. 48), the traditional chiefs in the Bamenda highlands and in the Muslim-dominated northern sections proved quite amenable to the administrative devolution envisaged by Britain's Governor-General for Nigeria, Sir Frederick Lugard.

Two key motifs of French colonial policy animated the administration of their Cameroun mandate: (1) the *politique de protectorat* as it developed in practice and (2) the economic policy of *mise en valeur*. The *politique de protectorat* (protectorate policy) was the consequence of a shift in French colonial policy from assimilation (complete integration of indigenous peoples into French political, social, and economic life) to one of association (slow development of the indigenous community toward eventual assimilation, with separation of European and African communities until assimilation was achieved). In practice, even though the system provided for some minimal participation of Africans in the making of policy, it tended to maintain the political and cultural gap between the French and the assimilated African on the one hand and the so-called *sujets indigènes* (native subjects) on the other. One of the primary props of the system was the legal separation of the two groups, a separation of which the *indigénat,* a comprehensive set of violations and penalties which local French administrators could invoke almost at will and without control, was the key. The *indigénat* applied wholly to member of the *sujets indigènes* group. The practical consequence of the system was to retard the political advancement of the latter group, an end openly espoused by the administration. As one French commissioner put it: "It was not . . . the wish of the local Administration that too rapid progress should be made; it wished to prevent any disturbance of the balance in the organization of the native tribes, which were still backward, and whose evolution should proceed steadily and reasonably." [4]

The policy of *mise en valeur* (development), first elaborated by Colonial Minister Albert Sarraut in 1923, called for an extensive local economic development as the basis of fruitful relations between the colonies and metropolitan France.[5] Applied to Cameroun, the policy resulted in a fivefold increase of the territory's total trade between 1922 and 1938, a relatively successful weathering of the worst years of the depression, and a considerable enlargement of the social overhead (that is, infrastructure, education, and so on) and of the economy as a whole. Much of the success of the *mise en valeur* in Cameroun was due, however, to a heavy tax burden and the use of conscript or *corvée* labor reinforced by the *indigénat* system. This use of forced labor aroused a great deal of indignation abroad. As a result of the urging of the Permanent Mandates Commission of the League of Nations and the adverse publicity created by the situation, the French administration finally diminished its use of *corvée* labor in 1933, and abolished it altogether in 1952.[6] During the latter years

[4] Statement by Commissioner Marchand before the League of Nations' Permanent Mandates Commission, in *Minutes and Reports of the Fifteenth Session, Permanent Mandates Commission* (Geneva: League of Nations, 1929), p. 131.

[5] Albert Sarraut, *La Mise en valeur des colonies françaises* (Paris: Payot, 1923).

[6] See Vol. II of Raymond Leslie Buell's, *The Native Problem in Africa* (New York: Macmillan, 1928), for one of the sharpest such condemnations of forced labor in the Cameroons.

of the mandate, before the outbreak of World War II, the French had also instituted a number of important political reforms. These included the 1937 labor reforms, promulgated by the Popular Front government of Léon Blum, and the sponsorship of quasi-political groups such as the Cameroun's Jeunesse Camerounaise Française, formed in 1938. There is little question, however, that these reforms were motivated at least in part by the need to stimulate pro-French sympathies in Cameroun and to counter the possibility that Germany's massive propaganda for the return of its former colonies might undermine African support for the administration. In all, although the mandate saw Cameroun's economy develop significantly, it left as one of its less pleasant residues widespread ill will toward the French, an ill will that was translated into nationalist activity after the war.

THE TRUSTEESHIP PERIOD [7]

In 1946, following the demise of the League of Nations, the two Cameroon mandates were converted into trust territories under the United Nation's trusteeship system. By accepting the new system, both Britain and France undertook to honor the political objectives stated in Article 76 of the United Nations Charter: "Progressive development towards self-government or independence." Insofar as France was concerned, the commitment represented a new departure, radical as compared to its former policies but wholly in line with the new colonial policies

[7] The period of trusteeship is covered at length in David E. Gardinier, *Cameroon: United Nations Challenge to French Policy* (London: Oxford University Press, 1963), and Victor T. Le Vine, *The Cameroons from Mandate to Independence* (Berkeley and Los Angeles: University of California Press, 1964), pp. 131–214.

enunciated in the French constitution of 1946 and spelled out in the legislation which flowed from it. For both Cameroons, then, the postwar era involved rapid political change, resulting in the attainment of independence for the French Cameroun on January 1, 1960, followed by the merger of the Cameroun Republic with the former British Southern Cameroons in October 1961 and the creation of the Cameroon Federal Republic.

Under the system of classification developed in the French constitution of 1946, the French Cameroun became an "Associated State" within the French Union. Overriding control of the territory still remained in the hands of the French National Assembly, but Cameroun now sent representatives to both houses of the French national parliament, as well as to the various organs of the French Union. A representative assembly with limited, principally advisory powers was set up in Cameroun, and elections to the new assembly were held under a dual electoral roll in which the African registry was restricted.

Significantly, the assembly had an African majority from the start, one destined for rapid growth. A new assembly elected in 1952 did not enjoy greater powers but had substantially more African seats due to an increase in the African rolls of nearly fifteen times the 1946 registration. Under the sweeping reforms of the 1956 *loi cadre,* a new Cameroun assembly was elected for the first time under a single roll embracing an electorate of 1,752,902 voters, a figure more than three times that of the total registration in 1952. The terms of the 1956–1957 reforms gave the Cameroun assembly and government almost complete internal control.

The first Cameroun government was formed in 1957

with André-Marie Mbida as the Premier. A ministerial crisis in February 1958 forced the resignation of Mbida, and Ahmadou Ahidjo became the new Premier. Ahidjo at once entered into negotiations with the French government for still greater autonomy and the setting of a date for complete independence. During 1959, Cameroun enjoyed complete internal self-government, a prelude to the achievement of full independence on January 1, 1960. This, of course, is only a skeletal outline of the major steps toward independence; the flesh and blood of the story are provided by the rise and development of Cameroonian nationalism, which will be discussed later in this chapter.

Events in the British Cameroons were somewhat more complex but can also be traced in broad strokes as a preliminary to more detailed discussion. The terms of the trusteeship agreement for the British Cameroons permitted the continuation of the administrative union under whose terms the Southern Cameroons were administered from Enugu, the capital of Eastern Nigeria, and the Northern Cameroons from Kaduna, the administrative center of Northern Nigeria. When, in 1947 (under the "Richards Constitution") Nigeria became "regionalized," the Southern Cameroons became a province of the Eastern Region. With the reforms of Nigeria's "MacPherson Constitution" (1951), the Southern Cameroons sent thirteen elected members to the Eastern House of Assembly, among them Dr. Emmanuel M. L. Endeley. In the meantime, political sentiment was growing for greater Southern Cameroonian autonomy. In 1953, Dr. Endeley, then leader of the "Cameroons bloc" in the Eastern House, won a domestic election on the issue of separation from Eastern Nigeria. The Nigerian "Lyttleton Constitution," promulgated in

1954, recognized the Southern Cameroon's wishes and made it a "quasi-federal territory" (in effect, giving it regional status) with its own House of Assembly and Executive Council. Further, the Southern Cameroons sent six representatives to the Nigerian House of Representatives in Lagos and was guaranteed one ministry in the Nigerian government. The Northern Cameroons, whose spokesmen had expressed no desire for separation from the Northern Region, was given representation in the Northern Regional House of Assembly and House of Chiefs at Kadun, plus a Minister for the Northern Cameroons and a Consultative Committee for Northern Cameroons Affairs.

The Southern Cameroons House of Assembly met for the first time in October 1954, and Dr. Endeley was named Leader of Government Business. In 1957, after his electoral alliance had won a close election, Dr. Endeley was renamed Leader of Government Business, a title which he held until May 1958, when new constitutional arrangements came into force. Under the new system, the Southern Cameroons received ministerial government, and Dr. Endeley was named Premier. In January 1959, general elections in the Southern Cameroons resulted in the defeat of Dr. Endeley's coalition and a narrow victory for the party led by John N. Foncha, a schoolmaster from Bamenda, who had campaigned on a platform of unification of the two Cameroons. Foncha thus became Premier, succeeding Dr. Endeley.

In May of the same year, the United Nations General Assembly, at the end of a special "Cameroons session," recommended that separate plebiscites be held in the Northern and Southern Cameroons to decide their respective political futures. The one in the north was scheduled to take place that November, but the Assembly took no further action on a plebiscite for the Southern Cameroons, owing to unresolved differences between Foncha and Endeley over the date of the plebiscite and the questions to be put. By October, however, these two leaders had reached agreement on the issues, and in December the General Assembly set February 11, 1961, as the date for the plebiscite in the south and for a second plebiscite in the north. (The November plebiscite in the Northern Cameroons had resulted in a vote to defer decision on the political future of that part of the trust territory.)

The question posed in both Northern and Southern Cameroons was whether to join Nigeria—which had become independent in October 1960—or to unite with the Cameroun Republic. On February 11, 1961, polling took place without incident in the Southern Cameroons and resulted in an overwhelming vote for unification with the Cameroun Republic. In contrast, the voting in the Northern Cameroons of February 11 and 12 produced a sizable margin for joining Nigeria. The results of the plebiscites are shown in Table 1.[8]

[8] A full description of the plebiscites, including the breakdown in voting for all the Southern and Northern Cameroons electoral districts, is found in *Report of the United Nations Plebiscite Commissioner for the Cameroons under United Kingdom Administration, Plebiscites in the Southern and Northern Parts of the Territory, on 11 and 12 February, 1961*, UN Doc. A/4727 (New York, 1961), originally issued as UN Docs. T/1556/Appendix and T/1556/Appendix/Add. 1 and 2, dated April 11, 1961. The best general discussion of the UN plebiscites of 1959 and 1961 yet published is to be found in Claude E. Welch, Jr., *Dream of Unity: Pan-Africanism and Political Unification in West Africa* (Ithaca: Cornell University Press, 1966), pp. 216–241.

Table 1. Results of United Nations plebiscites in British Cameroons, February 1961

Area	For Cameroun Republic	For Nigeria	Total votes	Margins
Southern Cameroons	233,571	97,741	331,312	135,830
Northern Cameroons	97,659	146,296	243,955	48,637
Totals	331,230	244,037	575,267	

The unificationists' victory in the Southern Cameroons was even more substantial than that predicted by the most optimistic KNDP (Kamerun National Democratic Party) leaders. Some 83 per cent of those registered voted, and the "white box" (the unification alternative) received 135,830 more ballots than the "green box" [pro-Nigeria]. Although Endeley vowed that he would continue to fight "to the end," and though N. N. Mbile, deputy leader of the opposition Cameroons Peoples' National Convention, repeated his demands for a partition of the territory along ethnic lines, the decisiveness of the vote could not be challenged. "Reunification" had been achieved without bloodshed and in an unimpeachably democratic manner.

The Rise and Character of the Nationalist Movement

Cameroon nationalist sentiment developed first in the French Cameroun and then gradually found its way into the British Cameroons as it grew in strength and intensity. Two dominant themes in the growth of Cameroonian nationalism can be traced in each part of the Cameroon: (1) in the French Cameroun, Cameroon nationalism per se and its outgrowth, the demand for the "reunification" of the two Cameroons (to use Cameroun nationalist terminology); (2) in the British Cameroons, first, Southern Cameroonian separatism (from Nigeria) and later, under the impetus of ideas and pressures from the east, a mounting pressure in that territory for "reunification" with the French Cameroun.[9]

THE FRENCH CAMEROUN

Although a number of political parties from metropolitan France established branches in the French Cameroun after 1946 and several purely indigenous political groups had already arisen by then, it is fair to say that Cameroun nationalism dates from 1948. In April of that year the Union des Populations du Cameroun (UPC) was formed by Ruben Um Nyobé, a former government clerk active in the Cameroun's nascent trade-union movement, Dr. Félix Moumié, a medical officer recently returned from his studies at Dakar, and several other trade unionists and government employees. The UPC represented a new turn in Cameroun politics as it was both a political party and an ideological innovator. As a party, it drew its initial strength from the leadership of Cameroun's leftist trade unions and from among the more militant members of the older political groups. As an ideological innovator it was the creator and carrier of what was essentially a two-point nationalist program: the unification of the two Cameroons and rapid progress toward complete independence under

[9] Welch, *ibid.*, p. 159, contends that the idea of unification originated first among British Cameroonians. French-speaking Cameroonians contend the idea was first articulated on their side of the border. It is impossible to know for certain either way: what is sure is that it seems to have found expression in both French and British Cameroons about the same time—that is, between 1947 and 1949.

the terms of the United Nations Charter. Within two months the UPC became the Cameroun branch of the Rassemblement Démocratique Africain (RDA) and had begun to attract support from influential "traditional" organizations such as Ngondo (Douala) and Kumsze (Bamiléké).[10] By the time the first United Nations Visiting Mission arrived in Douala in November 1949, the UPC had become, by all odds, the best-organized political party in the French Cameroun.

The next five years saw the formation of a large number of political parties and organizations, including Louis Aujoulat's Bloc Démocratique Camerounais (BDC—the lineal precursor of the present Parti des Démocrates Camerounais, PDC), Charles Okala's Union Sociale Camerounaise (USC, which became the Parti Socialiste Camerounais), several traditional organizations converted into political parties by ambitious politicians, and a number of *partis de l'administration,* often organized specifically to counter UPC activity in one area or another. During this period, the UPC became increasingly frustrated. It found the French administration hostile, the other parties preempting its nationalist program for their own use, and its

[10] Ngondo designates the community councils which existed in the various Douala villages long before the twentieth century. The Ngondo mentioned here is the "traditional" council of Douala "notables," converted in the late 1940's into an organizational adjunct of the various political formations created by such leaders as Paul Soppo Priso. In the traditional Bamiléké social system Kumsze was one of two secret societies described by Hurault as "societies magic in character, practicing . . . rites designed to insure the fertility of the earth and to ward off malevolent influences" (J. Hurault, *La Structure sociale des Bamiléké* [Paris: Mouton, 1962], p. 105; translation is mine).

candidates unable to win seats in the Cameroun assembly. Its only successes lay abroad, where repeated appearances by Um Nyobé and Moumié before United Nations organs served to propagandize the UPC's position and to make friends for it among anti-French or anticolonial delegations at the UN.

Even though most Camerounian political parties by the beginning of 1955 had openly espoused both the goals of independence and reunification (with varying qualifications), the UPC had failed to gather much support and decided to turn from verbal extremism to more violent action. During May of 1955, the UPC launched a series of riots, demonstrations, and attacks on property and persons in Douala and Yaoundé and throughout the southwestern part of the country, apparently hoping to ignite a nation-wide insurrection. The attempt failed, having misfired in the north, and lost momentum in the southwest in the face of swift and harsh government countermeasures. The UPC and its affiliate organizations were banned in July, and soon thereafter its leaders fled into the British Cameroons to set up emergency headquarters at Kumba. In September, the UPC directorate split, one wing (Reuben Um Nyobé, president and founder of the UPC, and Theodore Mayi Matip, his principal lieutenant) returning to continue the fight as *maquisards* and the other (Félix-Roland Moumié, Ernest Ouandié, Abel Kingué) eventually (after 1957) taking refuge first in Khartoum, then in Cairo, and finally in Accra and Conakry.

Officially banned and its leaders either in exile or in the *maquis,* the UPC, paradoxically, dominated the political scene between 1955 and 1960 as it had never been able to do when it was legal and competed openly with its op-

ponents. The continuing rebellion inspired by the UPC—
initially among the Bassa in the Sanaga-Maritime region,
later spreading to the Bamiléké areas and to other western
sectors and recurring with sporadic violence in the principal towns—plus the UPC's propaganda campaign waged
from the halls of UN and through the facilities provided by the United Arab Republic, Guinea, and Ghana,
preoccupied both the French administration and the
remaining political parties. One of the consequences
of this preoccupation was the introduction of a third
theme as an article of nationalist faith, that is, "reconciliation" by bringing the rebellion to an end through rescind-
ing the ban on the UPC and including its leaders in the
government. Significantly, the downfall of the coalition
Mbida government in 1958 was due to the fact that Mbida
used excessively harsh measures to combat the UPC—or
so it appeared to many Camerounian leaders—that he had
not pursued "reconciliation" with sufficient vigor, and that
he had not pressed for early independence from France.
The new government headed by Ahmadou Ahidjo was
formed through an alliance of the Union Camerounaise
(UC) group in the assembly (composed primarily of Muslim Fulani from the north and controlling twenty-nine
seats) and the Mouvement d'Action Nationale Camerounaise (MANC) formerly in opposition, which included such
leaders as Paul Soppo Priso and Charles Assalé. MANC
had a general outlook that was at once vigorously nationalist and actively reconciliationist. A small group of
deputies (Paysans Indépendants), representing important
indigenous agricultural interests in the western areas,
completed the coalition.

Throughout 1958 sporadic violence broke out in the

southwest, and not even the death of Um Nyobé in September 1958 brought an end to it. (It did end the Bassa phase of the revolt.) Throughout 1958, the external wing of the UPC, from Cairo, Conakry, and Accra, continued to stoke the fires of unrest in the countryside and in the principal towns to such an extent that substantial portions of the southwest became economically paralyzed. Moreover, the UPC kept up constant agitation at the United Nations and almost managed to convince that body that general elections—in which it expected to emerge victorious—should be held before independence was attained on January 1, 1960. With Guinean, Ghanaian, and Egyptian support, the UPC sought unsuccessfully to force itself into power by exploiting the unrest for which it had been largely responsible. It is interesting to observe that the only party which had the organization, the ideological dynamism, and the militant leadership to grow into an all-Cameroun movement dissipated its vitality by a premature attempt to seize power. The French Cameroun, then, attained independence not under the aegis of a national movement such as the Convention People's Party in Ghana or the Tanganyika African National Union, but in the care of a loose coalition of regional and ethnic-based parties into whose hands power had been thrust almost by default.

THE BRITISH CAMEROONS

In the British Cameroons, nationalist sentiment developed only in the Southern Cameroons, where longer contact with modern ways and a relatively good educational system had developed considerable popular political sophistication. The observation holds true even in the face of minor political party activity in the Northern Cameroons during the November 1959 plebiscite campaign and thereafter up to the February 1961 plebiscite. This activity had limited aims quite obviously connected with the alternatives posed in the two plebiscites and cannot be said to represent anything like a continuing political tradition. In this context, the two threads of Cameroons nationalism, separatism and reunification, can be traced in outline in the British Southern Cameroons.

The first steps in the direction of a Cameroons nationalism were probably taken in 1940, with the formation of the Cameroons Youth League (CYL) in Lagos by Peter M. Kale and Dr. E. L. M. Endeley. This organization did not have, at first, overtly political aims; like similar associations in Cameroon, its principal purposes were solidaristic and welfare oriented. Kale, together with L. N. Namme and N. N. Mbile, participated in the founding of Dr. Nnamdi Azikiwe's National Council of Nigeria and the Cameroons (NCNC), and were at various times members of the party's national executive. In 1946 the Cameroons mandate was converted into UN trusteeship, and Dr. Endeley returned home to plunge into local politics. He reactivated and politicized several semimoribund Bakweri tribal unions and, in 1947 brought the CYL and several tribal associations into a new group, the Cameroons Federal Union (CFU). The 1947 "Richards Constitution" failed to create a separate Cameroons region (as the CFU had demanded), and in late 1947 Dr. Endeley, already heavily involved with the CFU, joined with N. N. Mbile to assume the leadership of the Cameroon Development Corporation Workers' Union. The embers of separatism were kept glowing during 1948 and 1949 by the CYL (with

NCNC backing), and the CFU. In 1948 the CFU added "unification" of the two Cameroons to its demand for Southern Cameroons autonomy. There was even a motion by the Cameroons provincial council in Victoria demanding a separate region. The year 1949 also saw the formation of the Cameroons National (CNF) by Dr. Endeley, Mbile, Solomon T. Muna, and Sampson A. George.

By 1951 the CNF had become the Kamerun National Congress (KNC) and Endeley its president. Also in 1951, meetings in Kumba in August and December first brought the UPC and Southern Cameroons nationalist groups together. Dr. Endeley led the Southern Cameroons' representatives to the Eastern Nigerian House of Assembly in 1951 and 1953, as well as the Cameroons' delegation to the constitution conferences of 1953 and 1954. Still pursuing regional autonomy, Endeley and his delegation in 1953 won a virtual promise of regional separation if Endeley should win a general election at home on the issue of separation from Eastern Nigeria. In December 1953, the KNC won twelve of the thirteen seats to the Eastern House (the other went to the Kamerun Peoples' Party, KPP, a splinter from the KNC), and the 1954 "Lyttleton Constitution" provided quasi-federal status for the Southern Cameroons. In October, the Southern Cameroons House of Assembly met for the first time and Dr. Endeley was named Leader of Government Business. The first objective had been reached. The Southern Cameroons had achieved separate status within the federation. Developments within the French Cameroun, however, soon began to change the complexion of Southern Cameroonian politics.

The Southern Cameroons' unificationist strand must begin not only with Endeley but more particularly with the

person of Jabea K. Dibonge, a Douala from the French
Cameroun residing in Buea (Southern Cameroons) and for
many years a government clerk. In 1949 Dibonge organized
the French Cameroons Welfare Association [11] among the
Douala residing in the Southern Cameroons. Dibonge was
interested in strengthening Douala solidarity and mobiliz-
ing the French Camerounian workers on the Southern
Cameroons plantations. That same year the UPC, embold-
ened by the success of Ewe irredentist propaganda at the
United Nations debates over Togo, launched a full-fledged
campaign in the French Cameroun for unification, and the
UPC leadership lost no time in securing Dibonge's cooperation. It was 1955, however, that saw unification emerge
as a fully fledged nationalist goal in the Southern Cameroons. Two important events were responsible. First was
the formation of the Kamerun National Democratic Party
(KNDP), led by a Bamenda schoolteacher, John N. Foncha,
with a program of complete secession from Nigeria and, as
a long-range possibility, unification with the French Cameroun. Second was the appearance of the UPC directorate
at Kumba following the party's abortive revolt in the
French Cameroun.

Almost from the first, the KNDP cooperated with the
UPC and its youth and women's affiliates. The two parties,
meeting in Bamenda in November 1955, formed a "reunification committee," which functioned only briefly. It
was not long, however, until the more conservative KNDP
leadership became disenchanted with the extremism of
the UPC: the UPC demanded immediate independence

[11] Not to be confused with the Cameroons Welfare Union, formed
in Victoria in 1939. Its Lagos branch was the nucleus from which the
Cameroons Youth League was formed.

and reunification, a position considerably removed from the views of Foncha and his colleagues, who wanted a continuation of the trusteeship until future developments might make reunification possible. In 1957 the UPC was banned in the Southern Cameroons and its leaders deported, leaving behind a rump party, the One Kamerun (OK) headed by Ndeh Ntumazah. The March 1957 general elections in the Southern Cameroons resulted in a narrow loss for Foncha (KNDP, 5 seats; KNC, 6 seats; KPP, 2 seats), and the KNDP—as well as the OK, with which the KNDP leadership declined to be identified—continued to agitate for reunification.

In 1958, Ahmadou Ahidjo, a partisan of unification, became Premier of Cameroun, and France announced that it was prepared to grant its trust territory its independence on January 1, 1960. Both events strengthened the hand of the unificationists in the Southern Cameroons. In January 1959, the KNDP won fourteen seats in the enlarged House of Assembly, while the KNC-KPP took twelve. The stage was now set for the 1959 dialogue, conducted both at home and in the UN, to decide the ultimate fate of the entire British trust territory.

After the United Nations General Assembly decided in the spring of 1959 that separate plebiscites would be held in the two portions of the British trusteeship, Foncha and Endeley were unable to agree on the questions to be put. Endeley had now come full circle from advocating separation from Nigeria and eventual union with the French Cameroun to favoring integration with Nigeria as a regional component of the federation. He wanted an early plebiscite offering clearly stated alternatives. Foncha asked for immediate separation from Nigeria and—in somewhat of a retreat from his ardent unificationist position—an extension of the trusteeship until the political courses of the Southern Cameroons' two neighbors became clear. Then, he urged, two plebiscites should be held to decide the territory's attachment.

Under pressure from a number of African states at the United Nations in the fall of 1959, Foncha finally agreed to an early plebiscite, to be held between September 1960 and April 1961, that would pose a clear choice between joining an independent Nigeria or uniting with the Cameroun Republic. Throughout 1960, Foncha met with Ahidjo to discuss the shape of a future union, but little came of the talks except the vague outlines of a loose federal union. His party, however, began to campaign vigorously against the Nigerian alternative. Endeley, for his part, undertook to convince the electorate that its only rational choice lay with Nigeria, and he strove to magnify the point that union with the Cameroun Republic meant getting involved in the sanguinary troubles of that country. Foncha and his party played on local fears of Ibo domination (many Eastern Nigerians, including some Ibo, had already come to pose an economic threat to indigenous Southern Cameroonians) and the prospects of profitable union with ethnically related "brothers" (the relationship is rather limited, in fact). The plebiscite unequivocally resolved the issue. The advocates of unification won resoundingly in the south, as already noted, but lost by a considerable margin in the north (Table 1).

Independence and Unification: Republic into Federation

The results of the plebiscite in the Southern Cameroons were received with joy in the Republic, and Foncha became the hero of the hour. In contrast, the Republic took the results in the Northern Cameroons with ill grace. It claimed at the United Nations that Great Britain and Nigeria had exerted undue pressure on the northern electorate to the extent, for example, of bringing in 700 armed Nigerian policemen to coerce the voters into voting for Nigeria.[12] The importance of the complaint, it may be added here, was not that the Cameroun government thought that the plebiscite had been badly conducted but that it was genuinely disappointed at losing the Northern Cameroons as a strong card in the bargaining with Foncha over the status of the Southern Cameroons in the new federation. It is also possible that the Northern Cameroons were also seen as a political counter to the threat posed to the UC by the supposedly strong pro-UPC groups in the Southern Cameroons. Without the north, the Ahidjo government realized that Foncha's hand would be strengthened and that his demands for maximum local autonomy for his part of the federation would be difficult to deny. The Ahidjo government pursued its complaint in the United Nations; on April 21, 1961, the General Assembly rejected the Cameroonian allegations and voted to ratify the northern plebiscite by calling for the end of trusteeship and the inclusion of the Northern Cameroons territory into Northern Nigeria. Rebuffed by the General Assembly, the Cameroun government took its case to the World

[12] Republic of Cameroun, Ministry of Foreign Affairs and Secretariat of State for Information, *Position of the Republic of the Cameroun Following the Plebiscite of the 11 and 12th February 1961 in the Northern Portion of the Territory of the Cameroon under the Administration of the United Kingdom of Great Britain and Northern Ireland* (Yaoundé: The Ministry, 1961): "It is impossible to talk of self-determination when voters go to the polls at bayonet point" (p. 17 and *passim*).

Court; the move was more symbolic protest than substantive complaint, since the Court would take at least two years to render a verdict. (In December 1963, the Court refused to decide on the merits, contending that the General Assembly had already settled the issue.) [13] The new partners' mutual footdragging cut down the amount of time left for negotiation on the shape of the new federation. Two conferences, one in Foumban in July, and one in Yaoundé in August, eventually produced a constitutional text by the beginning of September.

On October 1, 1961, the two Cameroons were united and trusteeship over the British Southern Cameroons came officially to an end. The Northern Cameroons' trusteeship status had terminated on June 1, 1961, with the formal attachment of that portion of the territory to Nigeria. The Northern Cameroons became thenceforth the Sardauna Province of the Northern Region. Following the end of the trusteeship in the south, the former British Southern Cameroons became West Cameroon, and the Cameroun Republic was designated East Cameroon.

Some federal structures—the executive (with full decree and ordinance-making powers), the administrative machinery, and the security forces—went immediately into operation. By July 1962, the federal legislature had come into being: of fifty seats, ten were allocated to West Cameroon, and the rest to the eastern state. Ahidjo became federal President, and Foncha the Vice-President of the fed-

[13] International Court of Justice, *Reports of Judgements, Advisory Opinions and Orders, Judgement of 2 December 1963* (The Hague: I.C.J., 1964), pp. 33–34. Pleadings are documented on *International Court of Justice Pleadings, Northern Cameroons,* (The Hague: I.C.J., 1963).

eration. Foncha also retained his post as Prime Minister of West Cameroon as a result of the KNDP's decisive victory in the West Cameroon general elections held in January 1962. In addition, a full team of federal ministers was named, with five major posts going to West Cameroonians.

CHAPTER 2

The Contemporary Setting

Geography

Cameroon is roughly 700 miles long, approximately the size of California, and resembles in shape an irregular triangle with its apex touching Lake Chad and its base resting approximately on the line of two degrees north latitude. Cameroon is bounded on the south by Equatorial Guinea, Gabon, and the Peoples Republic of Congo (also known as Congo/Brazzaville), to the east by Chad and the Central African Republic, and to the west by Nigeria. A part of the Cameroon triangle's western side is bounded by the Bight of Biafra, the easternmost reach of the Gulf of Guinea. The coastline is dominated by Mount Cameroon, 13,360 feet in elevation and the highest mountain in west Africa. Mount Cameroon, an occasionally active volcano, is the southernmost peak of an irregular chain of mountains and rocky hills along the western border extending north by northeast virtually to the edge of Lake Chad.

The Federal Republic can be roughly divided into five geographic zones on the basis of dominant topographic, climatic, and vegetative features:

(1) The western mountain region contains, from north to south, Mount Cameroon, the Manengouba, Bambouto, and Mbam massifs (which include most of the Bamenda, Bamiléké, and Mambilla highlands), and comprises por-

tions of the Atlantika Hills, and, north of the Benue River, some of the Mandara Hills.

(2) The coastal forest plain extends from ten to fifty miles inland to the edge of the plateau of the inland forest region. This coastal region is very hot and humid and in it may be found some of the wettest places on earth, particularly on the seaward slopes of Mount Cameroon, where annual rainfall of over thirty feet has been recorded at Debundcha.

(3) The inland forest plateau, dominated by the tropical rain forest, lies on the average some 1,500 to 2,000 feet above sea level and extends about 300 miles to the northernmost edge of the rain forest. This area it is less humid than the coast, but daytime temperatures are as hot.

(4) Running east-west, the Adamawa Plateau region is in fact an extension of the mountain region. Average elevation is around 3,400 feet. The plateau region varies between 50 and 150 miles in width and tends to have a relatively pleasant climate. There is a fairly abrupt transition between the plateau and the northern savannahs.

(5) The northern savannah plain extends from the Adamawa Plateau region to Lake Chad, with the principal vegetation either scrub or grass cover. Humidity decreases and temperatures increase as one moves north.

The main rivers of Cameroon are the Wouri, near whose mouth Douala is located; the Sanaga; the Dja-Ngoko, flowing southwest into the Congo River; the Logone, draining into Lake Chad and forming part of the northwestern frontier; and the Benue, the eastern extension of the Niger. Garoua on the Benue is accessible from Lagos for about six weeks during the rainy season (July 15–September 15), making it one of the most important ports of the country. Other ports are Douala, the country's principal seaport; Kribi, an important port during the German period but now in some decline; and Tiko and Victoria-Bota, both in West Cameroon and that state's principal outlets to the sea.

The Economy

RESOURCES AND POTENTIAL RESOURCES

An objective assessment of Cameroon's natural resources cannot support much optimism that the Federal Republic will ever become significant as an economic power, even in west Africa. Its principal resources are those which will permit it to expand and exploit its agricultural sector. Its limited industry—with one important exception, the aluminum plant at Edéa—has been and undoubtedly will continue to be tied to agriculture. Nevertheless, despite a setback in 1965 due to a drastic decline in the international cocoa market price, the country's economy has been usually healthy and has, since 1960, continued to grow at a higher rate than that of any other west and equatorial African state except the Ivory Coast.

Soils and climate in the southern parts of East and West Cameroon encourage intensive cultivation of plantation crops such as cocoa, coffee, and bananas. These products, as a matter of fact, have long constituted the state's principal cash crops. An area of considerable present and potential growth has been the timber reserves of the tropical forest, an area estimated (in the East) to cover some 39,536,000 acres, of which, however, only some 4,942,000 are accessible under present conditions.

The main rivers are a source of potential hydroelectric power. But it is unlikely that, except for expansion of the

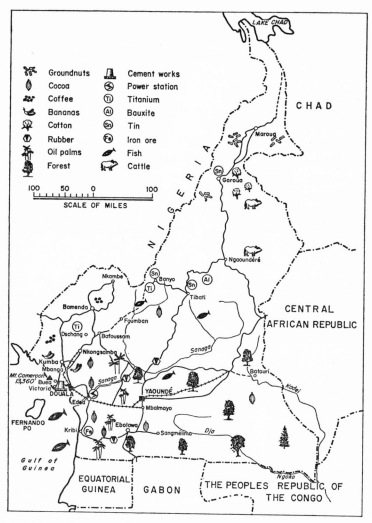

Map 2. Economic Resources, Cameroon Federal Republic.
(Adapted from *Africa 69/70* [Paris: *Jeune Afrique,* 1969], p. 231.)

existing facilities at Edéa and the development of a few hydroelectric stations to provide additional power for the towns, the growth of industry will ever be sufficient to warrant large-scale utilization of that potential.

Finally, a word must be said about minerals. Cassiterite and gold are mined in such small amounts as to be unimportant to the economy. An exceptionally large deposit of bauxite was discovered in 1959 at Martap, on the Adamawa Plateau, near Tibati. Recent surveys claim that it is over one billion tons, with a 44 per cent assayed proportion of recoverable alumina. The deposit is too far, however, from the coast (approximately 500 miles from Edéa, where it would have to be processed) to be presently exploitable. It is possible that, with the completion of the Transcameroon Railway to Ngaoundéré, the deposit will become accessible for development. That day, however, is still considerably in the future; best estimates suggest 1975 as the earliest date at which work would begin on the trunk line from Ngaoundéré to Tibati, given full financing of the project. There is also the question whether it will be economically worthwhile to bring the bauxite to Edéa in view of the proximity of other large deposits (in Guinea and Ghana) to seaports, where they will be much more readily exploitable.

ORGANIZATION OF THE ECONOMY

Except in some areas, the economies of the two Cameroons, separate for over forty years, have not yet sufficiently meshed to the extent that it is possible to speak except in the most general terms of an economy of the Federal Republic. What has been done toward integrating the economies of the two states, however, has been quite impressive and suggests that maximum effort is being expended to that end. Among the more significant of these developments are: introduction of the CFA franc [1] as common currency in both states; the promulgation of federal budgets in which joint East-West state enterprises are funded; the opening of a branch of the Cameroon Development Bank (a federal development-loan agency) in West Cameroon; the introduction in 1964 of the metric system in West Cameroon; the expansion of interstate air services; the completion in 1969 of a rail link from Mbanga (East Cameroon) to Kumba (West Cameroon), which has given the long isolated interior of West Cameroon access to the sea; the decision to unite the modernized coastal belt of East Cameroon with that of West Cameroon, making Tiko and Victoria-Bota subports of Douala; the opening in 1969 of the first practical road link between Douala and the Tiko-Victoria-Buea complex, reducing an all-day drive to two hours (56 kilometers); the creation of statistical services in West Cameroon, which made possible the elaboration of a new national plan that included developmental projections for the country as a whole.

During the first five years of reunification, West Cameroon underwent considerable economic dislocation, owing in part to the loss of Commonwealth preference (1963), in part to budgetary difficulties, and most, perhaps, to the

[1] The "CFA franc" is the standard currency of the French-speaking African states. CFA stands for Communauté Financière Africaine. The Franc zone, a monetary organization based on the French franc, covers monetary transactions in countries using the CFA franc. In 1971 the CFA franc was converted at the approximate rate of 275 CFA to the U.S. dollar.

shift from dependence upon Nigeria and Britain to dependence upon East Cameroon. Among other effects of reunification was a sharp rise in the price of most basic commodities which followed the introduction of the CFA franc
as standard currency in West Cameroon. For a time, West
Cameroon leaders had cherished the illusion that some
measure of economic independence would be possible
within the federation: the realities proved otherwise. The
new links between the states, then, have not only had the
effect of creating the outlines for a federal economy, but—
even more important for the West Cameroon—have finally
put an end to that state's long economic and political
isolation.

The economy of the Federal Republic is based almost
entirely upon agriculture. The predominant pattern is
subsistence farming, though a not inconsiderable portion
of the agricultural sector is devoted to the production of
exportable crops. Manioc, millet, cassava, and various
tuberous vegetables are the principal crops produced almost
exclusively for local consumption. Whereas palm oil produced in the East Cameroon is mainly consumed locally,
that which is produced in the West Cameroon constitutes
that state's fifth most valuable export crop. Peanuts and
bananas, which are important items in the local diet, are
also produced in both states in important quantities for
export. During 1968 coffee was the most important export
crop of both West and East. The major exports of the East
are cocoa and coffee, which together in 1968 accounted for
over 56 per cent of that state's exports. East Cameroon also
exported cotton, wood, rubber, meat, and livestock in
significant quantities; West Cameroon has important exports of wood, rubber, and palm kernels.

In East Cameroon, cocoa and bananas were, until recently, by far the dominant export crops. During the last decade, however, the production of bananas has declined for a number of reasons—among them, crop diseases and terrorist activity in the principal banana-growing areas—while cocoa output has increased. At the same time, coffee production has increased prodigiously. Forest products have become the third most important agricultural export, and cotton now ranks high as an export commodity. Thus, the structure of the economy, though still remaining oriented toward agriculture, has in fact changed remarkably over the past several years. To a large extent, these increases in output were preceded by significant improvements in the transportation system, which opened up new areas for production on a large scale. Unlike the traditional money crops of cocoa and bananas, which are still largely in the hands of Africans who organize production as a family enterprise, the export crops, such as cotton and coffee, whose production is soaring, are now organized on a plantation basis. Many agricultural experts believe that it would be possible to achieve similar progress in the traditional crops such as cocoa if improved methods of cultivation, harvesting, and processing are used. Cocoa production now averages only 350 kilograms per hectare (1 hectare = 2.471 acres), but a few modern plantations are capable of producing 1,000 or more kilograms per hectare.

The export sector of West Cameroon's economy is dominated by the plantations located mainly in the coastal Victoria division. The plantations, of which the most important are those run by the Cameroon Development Corporation (a statutory agency), were originally started by the Germans following their original purchase of about 250,000 acres of land. About 70,000 acres of this land throughout the territory are now under cultivation. Bananas are the principal plantation crop, and in 1965 the plantations produced roughly 50 per cent of the bananas exported by West Cameroon. Rubber is the second most important product of the plantations and is expected eventually to replace bananas. Cocoa, the most valuable export crop, is grown almost wholly on native farms. Coffee is the state's second most important export, accounting for 21 per cent of the value of all exports in 1966. Other plantation crops are palm kernels, palm oil, and tea. However important the plantation sector is to West Cameroon's export market, peasant agriculture still dominates the economic picture. Sample data taken in 1951 suggest that there were at that time some 500,000 acres in peasant cultivation as against 70,000 in the plantation areas. The proportion still remains much the same. Further, as Kenneth Berrill warns, it is easy to overstress exported cash crops, and it should be recalled that about three-quarters of the output from native farms is consumed locally.[2]

Another aspect of West Cameroon's economy that deserves mention is the remarkable growth and effectiveness of the cooperative producing and marketing system. Between 1952 and 1957, membership in cooperatives increased fivefold, reaching 11,000, and the value of cooperative-grown produce grew to £3,000,000, a seventeenfold increase. During this period, the banana crop came to

[2] Kenneth Berrill, "The Economy of the Southern Cameroons under United Kingdom Trusteeship," mimeo. (Cambridge, Aug. 1960), p. 5. This is a special study commissioned by the Southern Cameroons government.

dominate the cooperative effort, with sales worth more than 60 per cent of the total receipts. As in the plantation sector, however, efforts are now being made to convince banana growers that slower-growing crops such as rubber offer them the most promising future.

Manufacturing industry is only of slight importance at the present stage of West Cameroon's development. The economy of East Cameroon, although still basically pre-industrial, contains a growing industrial sector. Its single important ornament is the aluminum-processing plant at Edéa, which in 1968 produced some 53,000 tons of raw aluminum, using bauxite from Guinea. In 1967 the plant's capacity was increased to 60,000 tons per annum. Other industries include two hydroelectric power plants (the main one, at Edéa, with a top output of 189,700 kilowatts, services at the Edéa plant and the Douala area) and seven smaller thermal power plants; several cotton mills (including the new Compagnie Industrielle du Cameroun—CICAM—textile complex, with factories at Garoua and Douala); four rice-shelling plants; a rubber latex plant; several plants extracting oils from peanuts, palm kernels, and the like; a cocoa-treatment plant; a bicycle factory, several breweries, a plastics factory, and a number of generally small, secondary industrial enterprises producing such items as cement, aluminum utensils, soap, clothing, beer, shoes, and cigarettes. In all, the outlook for a modest growth in the Cameroonian industrial sector is quite good; as in 1968, Cameroon already ranked as the third most industrially developed of all the French-speaking African states.[3]

[3] A concise survey of the industrial potential of Cameroon may be found in a United Nations study, *Industrial Development in*

LINES OF EXTERNAL TRADE

By the end of 1968, almost seven years after reunification, the main lines of a national economy had begun to emerge. Some of the earlier patterns still survived, however. Even though, for example, West Cameroon's external trade increasingly turned to France and the Common Market countries, which became that state's principal buyers of its bananas, rubber, and timber, Great Britain and the sterling zone remained the state's principal source of imports, providing 40 per cent of the total in 1967. It is expected, however, with the rail and road links between the two states finally completed, that the western state's trade will move more rapidly from its traditional British patterns.

The overall pattern of trade is still, as was the case before federation, weighted heavily toward French and Common Market channels, both in value and volume. France is Cameroon's principal market for its bananas, cotton, and coffee. In 1960, the Netherlands supplanted France as the principal purchaser of cocoa and timber. Other important trading partners within the Common Market include West Germany, Italy, Belgium, and Luxembourg. Other important trading partners outside the Common Market are the United States, Switzerland, and Japan. Guinea is important in this regard, since most of

---

Africa, UN Doc. ID/CONF. 1/RPB/1, (New York, 1967), pp. 243–254. The entire Cameroon economy is well discussed in the International Monetary Fund's *Surveys of African Economies,* Vol. I (Washington, D.C.: I.M.F., 1968). The most recent analysis of the Cameroonian economy, published too late for use here, is *L'Economie camerounaise* (Paris: Ediafric, 1971).

the bauxite processed at Edéa comes from that country. Overall, however, France dominates the external trade of Cameroon; Table 2 shows the salient characteristics of this trade.

Table 2. Foreign trade

Direction of trade, 1969

Principal suppliers	% of total imports	Principal purchasers	% of total exports
(EEC, incl. France)	(69.9)	(EEC, incl. France)	(72.8)
France	50.5	France	32.1
Federal Germany	10.1	Netherlands	25.9
U.S.A.	6.0	Federal Germany	9.9
Italy	5.2	U.S.A.	5.9
Gabon	3.4	Italy	4.2
Guinea	3.0	Belgium-Luxembourg	2.1
Others *	21.8	Others †	19.9

Principal exports and imports, 1969
(in millions of CFA francs)

Imports	Value	Exports	Value
Machines and electrical equipment	8,664	Cocoa and by-products	22,833
		Coffee	11,828
Transport material	8,211	Aluminium	6,461
Textile materials	6,820	Timber and tropical	
Chemical products	6,099	woods	5,149
Metal goods	4,125	Cotton	3,040
Mineral products,		Bananas	1,540
including oil and		Rubber	1,111
lubricants	3,829	Oilseeds	936
Food and drink	3,314		

Table 2 (continued)

Comparative totals, 1967–1969 (in millions of CFA francs
and millions of U.S. dollars) ‡

Year	Imports	Exports
1967	46,759 ($190.8)	43,569 ($177.8)
1968	46,320 ($189.0)	48,622 ($198.4)
1969	53,000 ($209.5)	59,423 ($234.9)

* Includes Netherlands, Belgium, Japan, United Kingdom, and
Venezuela.
† Includes Spain, Guinea, Gabon, United Kingdom, and Japan.
‡ Indices of conversion: for 1967 and 1968, U.S. $1 = 245 CFA;
for 1969, U.S. $1 = 253 CFA. The 1969 conversion index was deter-
mined in consideration of the devaluation of the franc, which
affected the CFA franc in August 1969. Before August the rate was
245 CFA = U.S. $1; afterward it became 275 CFA = U.S. $1. The
formula for deriving the 1969 index was thus:

$$\frac{(245 \times 7) + (275 \times 5)}{12}$$

Sources: United Nations, Economic Commission for Africa, *Foreign Trade Statistics of Africa,* UN Doc. E/CN.14/STAT/SER.
A/10 (New York, 1968), Ediafic, *Afrique 1968* (Paris: Ediafic, 1968);
Africa Research Bulletin (Economic, Financial and Technical Series),
various issues, 1970.

DEPENDENCE ON OUTSIDE ECONOMIC AID

Kenneth Berrill concluded in 1960, prior to the plebiscite in the British Cameroons, that whichever way that
territory turned, it would still need an estimated £1,000,000
per annum to maintain its rate of economic growth.[4] The
key fact for West Cameroon is that its economy is far from
being viable, and if it is to move forward sizable injections

4 Berrill, *op. cit.,* p. 15.

of development capital are needed. Prior to unification, the United Kingdom, notably through its Colonial Welfare and Development Program, was mainly responsible for providing these funds. With unification, the United Kingdom gave the Southern Cameroons some £714,000 as a parting gift and extended Commonwealth preference for West Cameroon exports to September 1963. Although new development capital may still come from Great Britain, it is likely to be from private rather than public sources; the majority of the funds it needs will, therefore, have to come from its sister state and from public and private international sources. Various attempts were made to attract new capital during the first five years of unification, but what few gains were made in this area were offset by the problem of the recurrent budgetary deficits suffered by West Cameroon. The creation of a customs barrier on the Nigerian border, and the maintenance of a similar barrier with East Cameroon, resulted in revenue losses that forced a federal subvention to the West Cameroon budget that accounted for two-thirds of that state's revenue of approximately \$7,200,000 by 1964–65.[5] The internal customs barrier was removed in 1966, when the UDEAC tariffs were applied to West Cameroon.

French aid to East Cameroon after it attained independence continued virtually on the same level as before. During 1960 and 1961 this was estimated at about \$40,000,000, if such items as the salaries of French "technical counselors," French military aid, subsidies to Cameroonian students in France, and the like were included, as well as the

[5] Edwin Ardener, "The Nature of the Reunification of Cameroon," in Arthur Hazelwood, ed., *African Integration and Disintegration* (London: Oxford University Press, 1967), p. 317.

more obvious forms of aid such as direct subventions from
the French Treasury, loans, and grants. Budetary subsidies
from France came to an end in 1964–65; during that year,
Cameroon celebrated its first budget balanced without external assistance. By early 1971, there had been no resump-
tion of that form of aid. France, however, continues to be
the federation's chief source of foreign aid, followed closely
by the European Development Fund (an agency of the
Common Market). Table 3 summarizes the estimated
value of foreign aid to Cameroon from 1961 to 1965.

Table 3. Foreign aid to Cameroon, 1961–1965
(in millions of CFA francs)

Source	Amount
France	19,855
European Development Fund	14,122
US/AID	5,000
West Germany	2,120
Other	3,000
Total	44,097 *

* $183.7 million.

Source: United Nations, *Industrial Development
in Africa,* UN Doc. ID/CONF.1/RBP/1 (New
York, 1967), p. 254.

The conclusion is unavoidable: without massive foreign
aid, particularly French aid, the Cameroon Federal Republic cannot continue its present rate of development. In this
connection, it is interesting to note that East Cameroon's
twenty-year plan, prepared in 1959, estimated that 42 per
cent of the financing of the plan, at least for the first five
years (1961–1965), would have to come from "external

sources." [6] Substantial international aid has already been granted the new federation; for example, the northward extension of the Douala-Yaoundé railway (the Transcameroon Railway) was initially financed by a consortium of EEC, American, and French funding amounting to about $31,615,000.

Social Structure

ETHNIC DIVISIONS AND THEIR STRENGTH

The Cameroun Republic presents an unusually complex and fragmented ethnic picture. It has been estimated that there are more than 136 identifiable linguistic groupings in East Cameroon and about 100 vernaculars in West Cameroon. Neither state has had a complete census since unification; the last West Cameroonian count was part of the 1953 Nigerian census, and East Cameroon has never had a full census, either before or after independence. All population figures for the federation, therefore, are simply estimates based on partial or complete urban censuses, sample population surveys, and projections (in the case of West Cameroon) from the 1953 base figures.[7] Given these reservations, the United Nations suggests a combined population figure of about 5,470,000 for mid-1967, an estimate more than 400,000 above its 1966 figure (5,017,000).

[6] [Société Générale d'Etudes et de Planification, for the] Ministry of the Plan, Republic of Cameroun, *Plan de développement économique et social,* Vol. I, *Rapport general* (Paris and Yaoundé: The Ministry 1960), pp. 37–40.

[7] It should be noted that the 1953 figures are by no means above suspicion, since the 1963–1964 Nigerian censuses suggested that the earlier count was off by as much as 60 per cent in some localities. The former British Cameroons was not included in the 1963–1964 enumerations because it had by then become West Cameroon.

The latter estimate is the more reliable, however, since it is based on partial censuses completed in 1965. Those surveys gave West Cameroon a population of 1,030,720, East Cameroon, 3,987,000.[8]

Similar problems obtain for any attempt to list the principal ethnic groups in Cameroon. Not only are the systems of classification often mutually contradictory, but given the fact that many of the ethnic lines have become quite blurred over time, it is virtually impossible to make such a listing without treading on various anthropologists' and ethnographers' toes.[9] A nominal listing of the principal groups, however, with some estimate of numerical size can be constructed (Table 4).

Among the southern Nigerians, who are found mainly in West Cameroon, the aggressive and commercially adept Ibo, numbering some 25,000, have been the most important. The Ibo have tended increasingly to dominate the petty commerce of West Cameroon and are, as a consequence, resented by many indigenous West Cameroonians. A measure of the importance of this fact is that the threat of Ibo domination was skillfully utilized by Premier Fon-

[8] United Nations, *Demographic Yearbook, 1967* (New York: UN, 1968), p. 98; *La population du Cameroun occidental* (Yaoundé: Imprimerie Nationale, 1965).

[9] On the basis of a variety of sources, including a basic classificatory system suggested by George P. Murdock in his *Africa: Its Peoples and Their Culture History* (New York: McGraw-Hill, 1959), I attempted to put together a listing of the principal groups in both Cameroons in *The Cameroons from Mandate to Independence* (Berkeley and Los Angeles: University of California Press, 1964), pp. 12–14. But see Ardener's critique of some aspects of that classification in "The Nature of the Reunification of Cameroon," *op. cit.*, pp. 294–299.

Table 4. Major ethnic groups in Cameroon, 1967

Groups	West	East
Cameroon Highlanders (Bamiléké, Tikar, Bamun, etc.)	400,000	900,000
Equatorial Bantu (Beti-Fang)	n.d.*	773,000
Northern Negroid pagans ("Kirdi")	n.d.	600,000
Fulani (Foulah, Peuhl, etc.)	n.d.	450,000
Northwestern and Coastal Bantu (Bassa-Bakoko, Douala, etc.)	24,000	267,000
Eastern Nigritic (Baya, Mboum, etc.)	20,000	248,000
Southern Nigerian (Ibo, Ibibio, Efik, etc.)	155,000	n.d.
Islamized pagans and Chadic	n.d.	120,000
Plateau Nigerians	12,500	28,000
Pygmy	n.d.	6,500

* n.d. = no data, or in such small numbers as to be insignificant.

cha and the KNDP as an argument for unification with the Cameroun Republic during the February 1961 plebiscite. Other southern Nigerians include Efik, Ibibio, Ekoi, Anyang, Boki, Edo, Tiv, and Ijaw.

The Northwestern and Coastal Bantu comprise a group of important ethnic units including the Douala, presently about 50,000 strong and the first Cameroonians to be subject to Western influences, and the Bassa-Bakoko, a grouping of about 200,000 occupying the general area of the Sanaga River Valley. The Bassa, it will be recalled, were the first of the southern ethnic groups to participate in the political violence which began in 1955.

The most important numerical component of the Equatorial Bantu is the so-called Beti-Fang (also known as the Beti-Pahouin) agglomerate, a widely dispersed grouping which includes the tribes inhabiting the Yaoundé area.

The principal dialects of the agglomerate are Ewondo (470,000 speakers), Bulu (130,000), and Fang (48,000).

Pygmies, thought once to have been the original inhabitants of the southern forest area, are now dispersed in small villages and isolated in the equatorial forest of the southeast.

The largest ethnic grouping in Cameroon is that of the "Cameroon Highlanders," composed principally of the Bamiléké (about 800,000); the various related tribes of the Bamenda Plateau, most of them of Tikar origin (about 400,000); and the Bamun (85,000). Most Bamiléké live in the several Bamiléké administrative divisions on the East-West border, but over 100,000 have emigrated to take up residence elsewhere in the two Cameroons. The largest number of Bamiléké emigrants are found in the towns of East Cameroon. The various Tikar tribes are also known as "grassfielders," after the characteristic cover of the Bamenda highlands, a name that is also often used by the Bamiléké. The Bamun are of particular interest because they represent a cultural development differing greatly from that found among the Bamiléké and Tikar. The Bamun were Islamized and have enjoyed what they claim is an unbroken dynastic monarchical rule through forty-four descendants of their founder. The Bamun also boast a remarkable Sultan, Njoya, who at the turn of the twentieth century invented a written language and had a history of his people inscribed in it.

Plateau Nigerians, eastern Nigritic tribes, and the so-called Kirdi are different agglomerates of what are essentially numerous small communities of animist peoples living in the western hills or, in the case of the Kirdi (*kirdi* is the Fulani term for "pagan"), both as hill dwellers and as nomads on the plains of the Logone. Most of these peoples are quite primitive, particularly the Kirdi, the majority of whom still reject clothing and tend to shy away from modernizing contacts. In recent years, however, Christian missionairies have made many converts among the Kirdi.

The Islamized pagans and the Chadic peoples are found mainly near Lake Chad. The principal groups of the latter classification are the Shuwa (Choa) Arabs, the Kanuri, and the Hausa.

Finally, the Fulani, of which there are some 450,000 in Cameroon, are mainly pastoralists and represent the dominant ethnic group in the north. Fulani emirates, lamidates (a chiefdom ruled by a *lamido,* or Fulani chief), and sultanates of the Cameroon north derive from the Fulani conquests of the Chad plain at the beginning of the nineteenth century. The principal towns of the Cameroon north, such as Maroua, Garoua, and Ngaoundéré, owe much of their importance to the fact that they are also capitals of chiefdoms.

DEGREE AND IMPACT OF URBANIZATION

Cameroon's first contacts with the West were along the coast, and it was natural that the early coastal trading centers should have been the nuclei around which Cameroon's first urban centers grew. The burgeoning coastal towns, as nexuses of the Western exchange economy, fostered the growth of trade and, in the process, created an elite based on nontraditional values (mechanical skill, education, money, and so on), and thereby hastened the breakdown of traditional social structures. The new townsmen could assert their independence from their traditional

milieus and, in so doing, escape from the ancient hier-
archies of status and birth. This dissociation completed the
breakdown of the Douala political system and is well on
its way to destroying that of the Yaoundé (Beti) group.
In point of time, of course, Douala, as the site of the first
European trading activity along the Cameroon coast, was
the first Cameroonian town to receive the full impact of
the Westernization process, though Victoria, historically
the first permanent European settlement, was founded as
late as 1858. Yaoundé was not occupied by Europeans until
after 1890, when the Germans opened a station there.
Other trading stations, such as Edéa, Tiko, Kribi, and
Nkongsamba, grew into towns only after the Germans had
converted them into commercial centers or ports. Douala
became, after 1884, the largest town in the Cameroon and
remains so today. Table 5 gives the current estimated
population of the principal Cameroon towns.

Two related sets of problems illustrate the continuing
difficulties faced by the Cameroon's urban centers: (1) the
relative sociodemographic and economic decline of the
indigenous population of the towns in the face of the
increasingly numerous immigrant populations and (2) the
complex social and economic problems caused by the growing inability of the towns to absorb the influx. These are, of
course, problems that are common to many urban centers
in Africa; what makes them crucial in Cameroon is that
the situations they create have promoted recruitment to
extremist political causes and thereby undermined attempts to solve them. Three Cameroon towns, Douala,
Yaoundé, and Kumba, serve as useful examples.

Douala is Cameroon's largest town, its principal port,
and its most important commercial center. Its urban social

Table 5. Principal Cameroon urban centers, 1967 (estimated population)

West Cameroon		East Cameroon	
City	Population	City	Population
Kumba	40,000	Douala	200,000
Tiko	15–20,000	Yaoundé	98,000
Victoria-Bota	15,000	Nkongsamba	39,800
Mamfe	12,000	Garoua	30,000
Bamenda	10,000	Foumban	18,000
Buea	5,000	Maroua	18,000
		Dschang	15,000
		Ebolowa	15,000
		Ngaoundéré	15,000
		Bafoussam	8,600
		Sangmélima	7,500
		Eséka	6,600
		Batouri	6,000
		Edéa	6,000
		Mbalmayo	5,500
		Kribi	3,200

problems are also the most serious. One cause of this fact is the change in the ethnic composition of the town, a change due principally to the influx of workers from the north and east. In 1947, the town had a population of 51,077, and the Douala, the original inhabitants, made up 46 per cent of the total (22,927). The Bassa, Bamiléké, and Beti then represented respectively only 14.9, 16.3, and 16.3 per cent of the population. In 1955–1956, official census figures revealed that the pattern had changed considerably. The Douala had not increased to any measurable degree (they then numbered 23,073) but they now constituted only 20.4 per cent of a total population of almost 125,000. Moreover, other ethnic groups had increased in size, particularly the Bamiléké, who with almost 30,000 now constituted 26.2 per cent of the total. The immigrants, unfortunately for the Douala, were aggressive and commercially vigorous and by 1956 had come to dominate petty trading and retailing, transportation, and most of the unskilled labor fields. They had even made inroads into the so-called learned trades (government service, mission work, education), at the expense of the local Douala who had formerly dominated these fields. Incidental to the influx of unskilled labor into Douala have been the growth of unemployment and the attendant problems caused by the presence of a large idle group. Government censuses in 1960 estimated that about 25,000 unemployed lived in Douala. One authority has pointed out that if the estimates include those who have never held a job, and hence have never been counted as "unemployed" on the censuses, approximately one-fourth, at a minimum, of the population of Douala is composed of men without visible means of support.[10] The presence of this unemployed mass undoubtedly contributed to the recurrence of UPC extremism and violence in Douala and to the fact that the UPC still commands a considerable degree of loyalty within the immigrant com-

[10] George Chaffard, "Cameroun à la veille de l'indépendance," *Europe-France-Outremer*, XXXVI, No. 355 (June 1955), 65. The figures and analysis derive from Etat du Cameroun, Service de la Statistique Générale, *Résultats de recensement de la ville de Douala (1955–1956): Population Autochtone.* (Yaoundé: Imprimerie du Gouvernement, 1957). More recent estimates suggest 150,000 urban unemployed for the country as a whole—for example, Philippe Hugon, *Analyse du sous-développement en Afrique noire: L'Exemple de l'Economie du Cameroun* (Paris: Presses Universitaires de France, 1968).

munity. The rapid growth of Douala, its large numbers of unemployed, and the prevalence of a good deal of ethnic tension among the *nouveaux arrivés* seems also to have contributed to the growth of prostitution and to widespread alcoholism in the town.

These problems are duplicated on a lesser scale in Yaoundé and Kumba. In Yaoundé, it is the Bamiléké again who represent the principal economic threat to the local Beti and who have taken almost complete control of petty trading and transport. Moreover, again a sizable group of unemployed continue to be a source of tension and political unrest. In Kumba, it is not the Bamiléké who constitute the principal threat but immigrant Ibo and others from Eastern Nigeria, who are just as aggressive and enterprising as the Bamiléké across the eastern border. Exact figures are not available, but it has been estimated that almost one-third of Kumba's population is Eastern Nigerian in origin. The Ibo have taken over much of the petty trading and, like the Bamiléké, tend to gather local private transport of goods and people into their own hands. The indigenous Cameroonians in Kumba resent these developments, and their resentment provided a political field which both the KNDP, with its anti-Ibo propaganda, and the extremist One Kamerun Party (OK) could plow with ease. It is significant to note that the Kumba area was one of the OK's principal strongholds and to recall that Kumba voted 5,349 to 719 (the Ibo, as non-Cameroonians, could not vote) in favor of unification at the February 1961 plebiscite.[11]

[11] I have discussed these matters at length in my book *The Cameroons from Mandate to Independence*, pp. 49–58.

At least one consequence of the influx of Bamiléké and Ibo into the towns has been a restructuring of the African social *milieu* that resulted in the newcomers' assuming leading, and often dominant, positions in the community. In another context, the Bamiléké and Ibo also exemplify the problems caused by large-scale extraurban migration in both Cameroon states.

The Bamiléké, found mainly in the five Bamiléké departments, number some 800,000, to which must be added another 100,000 who have taken up residence elsewhere in the East Cameroon, particularly in the larger towns. The wave of Bamiléké migration began and continues for a number of related reasons. The Bamiléké areas are overpopulated (up to 800 persons per square mile in some localities) in respect to the land traditionally available within these areas. Undivided inheritance of rights and property restricts the number of claimants on the land and forces the younger siblings of the named heir to found their own lines or to seek their fortunes outside the traditional areas. Tradition endows Bamiléké chiefs with considerable power over the land, inasmuch as the chief, who is considered to hold the land in trust for the tribe, has the authority to allocate usufructuary rights—though never ownership in the Western sense. The chiefs have tended to resist change and modern technology and often abuse their powers, at least in the eyes of the younger Bamiléké. The net result of this situation has been, over the years, a growing wave of migration from the Bamiléké areas, principally southward in the direction of Douala and eastward toward Yaoundé.

The emigrants, highly energetic and opportunistic by nature, gradually took economic control of the Mungo region between the Bamiléké area and Douala and have come to dominate the Douala area itself. Mention has already been made of their influence elsewhere in the Cameroon. An important by-product of the exodus has been the high level of politicization among the immigrants, a fact which has made them vocal opponents of government, of the old mores, and of the traditional Bamiléké chiefs and often willing recruits to the UPC *maquis*. When the Republic was created and large numbers of *maquisards* "returned to legality" following relegalization of the UPC, the government of Prime Minister Ahidjo secured the adherence of a group of Bamiléké deputies (most of them ex-UPC *maquisards*) and even made the group's leader, Pierre Kamdem Ninyim, an important *maquis* chief, a Minister of State. The move was interpreted, with justification, as an attempt to placate the younger Bamiléké dissidents, both in the Bamiléké areas and in the principal towns. Kamdem Ninyim was subsequently eased out of the cabinet, but only, apparently, when the government felt that the Bamiléké situation had become more manageable. He finally became implicated in the murder of an East Cameroon deputy and was executed in February 1963.[12]

Much of the tension underlying Bamiléké unrest had not been directly faced, however, by the East Cameroon

[12] At the time of his appointment he was, at twenty-four, the youngest cabinet minister in Africa. His responsibilities included health and population; many people who knew of his *maquis* background derisively styled him "le ministre de dépopulation et coupe-gorges" (the minister of depopulation and cut-throats).

government. Some administrative devolution has taken place, and most guerrilla bands have been gradually decimated due to stringent measures. But the basic problems concerning the use of Bamiléké land, the power of the chiefs, the progressive alienation of Bamiléké youth, and the frictions caused by Bamiléké emigration have yet to be fully confronted.

In West Cameroon almost continuous migratory activity seems to be the rule. Kenneth Berrill summarized the situation:

There is migration into the Bamenda Highlands by Northern Fulani seeking tse-tse-free grazing for their cattle; there are migrants from the over-populated villages of East Nigeria who come to provide labour both for plantations and peasant farms; there is migration within the Territory as Cameroonians move from the bush to the roads or from village to village in search of better land; and above all there is the now traditional migration from interior to coast of young men coming for a few years to work on the plantations and see something of a wider world.[13]

The process has produced a variety of tensions throughout the territory. Grasslanders on the northern fringes of the Bamenda Plateau have been in almost constant friction with the herding Fulani. Inhabitants of the southern portions of West Cameroon, particularly the Victoria division, are faced with Ibo-Ibibio economic penetration from the west and the presence of large numbers of grassfielders and Eastern Nigerians in the labor force of the plantations. The importance of these tensions, especially with regard to the Ibo, has already been noted, but it is

[13] Berrill, *op. cit.,* p. 2.

worth reiterating that the presence of immigrant outsiders in the territory was sufficiently threatening to be useful as political capital for two of the three major West Cameroonian parties (the Kamerun National Democratic Party and the Cameroons Peoples' National Convention).

MODERN SOCIAL AND ECONOMIC GROUPS

Almost all Cameroonian trade unions, with the exception of a few local ones, have played in the past and continue to play an important role in the political life of the country. Before 1963, when the main trade unions merged, wherever trade unionism was strong in East Cameroon—in the principal towns and in some plantations in the southwest—the unions had no hesitation about endorsing candidates, actively campaigning on behalf of parties, and even occasionally presenting candidates of their own under independent or new party labels. But, however important the labor organizations were to the formation of some parties or to the support of others, the influence of the trade-union movement by 1960 was still relatively small, even though it was estimated that in 1959, 26 per cent of East Cameroon's salaried labor force of about 135,000 had trade-union connections. By 1963, with the consolidation of East Cameroon political parties, four of the largest trade unions and several of the smaller ones (combined membership in 1965 was estimated at 60,000) had merged to form the Fédération des Syndicats du Cameroun, and the FSC itself thereupon became—despite the "autonomy" required by its statutes—the labor arm of the dominant Union Camerounaise (now Cameroon National Union) party. The merger also coincided with increased recruitment to trade-union ranks: in 1965, of the 150,000 wage earners in the country as a whole, more than 88,500 were claimed by trade unions (68,500 in East Cameroon; ca. 20,000 in West Cameroon).[14] However, what trade unionism exists is found mainly in the southern areas; almost none is found in the predominantly Muslim northern areas of East Cameroon.

Trade-union activity has always been significant in West Cameroon: in 1959, some 14,880 of the salaried labor force of 37,828 (39.3 per cent) were connected with trade-union organizations; in 1965, about 20,000 of the estimated 40,000 West wage earners were so affiliated. The two principal unions, the Cameroon Development Corporation Workers' Union (CDCWU) and the Likomba Plantation Workers' Union, have organized workers in the largest plantation enterprises in West Cameroon. In addition, some six other trade unions, organizing bank employees, commercial and clerical workers, postal and telegraph workers, various public employees, teachers, and nurses have become active since 1964. All trade unions except the nurses' are affiliated with the West Cameroon Trade Union Congress (WCTUC), formed in 1962. The WCTUC, like its brethren groups in East Cameroon and despite its heterogeneous ethnic composition, came in turn to be considered something of a political appendage of the dominant Cameroon National Union party, particularly since its merger with the two East Cameroon trade union federations in 1969 (see below). On the point of ethnic diversity, the Ardeners' and Warmington's 1960 study is quite

14 The estimate for wage earners is from the I.M.F. survey, *op. cit.* Data on trade-union membership are from U.S. Department of Labor, Bureau of International Labor Affairs, *Directory of Labor Organizations in Africa* (Washington, D.C., 1966), Vol. II, chap. vi.

revealing: in January 1958, of a total of 17,742 CDC workers enumerated, 11,426 originated in various parts of the British Cameroons, 5,414 came from Nigeria, 895 from the French Cameroun, and 7 from other African areas.[15] A similar ratio was found on the Likomba plantations of Elders & Pfyfe, a British firm with extensive holdings in West Cameroon. All West Cameroon labor organizations have, since unification, cut formal ties with their Nigerian parent organizations but the WCTUC retained it affiliation with the International Confederation for Free Trade Unions (ICFTU). Even though for a time the trade unions considered themselves to be apolitical, the CDCWU at least provided valuable training and no doubt furthered the political careers of such important politicians as Dr. E. M. L. Endeley, who was the first CDCWU president, and N. N. Mbile, who followed Endeley in that post. The process of organizational consolidation, whereby the principal trade unions merged into their present formations, is somewhat confusing and requires additional comment.[16]

The most useful point of departure is a recent event: in October 1969, Cameroon's three principal trade union

[15] Edwin Ardener, Shirley Ardener, and W. Alan Warmington, *Plantation and Village in the Cameroons* (London: Oxford University Press for the Nigerian Institute of Social and Economic Research, 1960), pp. 356–358.

[16] For an in-depth study of the CDC Workers' Union (CDCWU) see W. A. Warmington's excellent *A West African Trade Union* (London: Oxford University Press for the Nigerian Institute of Social and Economic Research, 1960). The following data are taken from U.S. Department of Labor, *Directory of Labor Organizations, loc. cit.;* I am also grateful for information on the Cameroonian labor situation kindly provided by Willard Johnson in a letter to me dated July 12, 1963.

Table 6. Principal modern social and economic groups in Cameroon

Name and type, by function	State	Affiliates	External connections	Membership claimed (last available figures)	Remarks
LABOR UNIONS*					
Fédération des Syndicats du Cameroun (FSC)	E	200 (six listed below)	ICFTU, African Trade Union Confederation (ATUC)	60,000 (1965)	Formed 1963 by merger of USLC, UGTC, CGCT, USAC (see text); supports and is supported by Cameroon National Union party
1. Union Nationale des Syndicats de Travailleurs Agricoles, Forestiers, Bois, Elevages, et Pêches du Cameroun (UN-ASABEC)	E	None	Formerly allied with UGTC	n.a.†	Formed 1960 by merger of two unions
2. Syndicat National des Employés de Banque au Cameroun (SNEBC)	E	None	None	1,000 (1966)	Formed 1965
3. Syndicat Professionnel des Employés du Commerce du Cameroun (SPEEC)	E	None	ITS-International Federation of Commercial, Clerical and Technical Employees	1,005 (1964)	
4. Section des Travailleurs Postaux	E	None	None	n.a.	

5. Syndicat des Postes et Communications (SPC)	E	None	ITS–Postal, Telegraph & Telephone International	350 (1962)	
6. Union Nationale des Cheminots du Cameroun (UNCC)	E	None	None	2,000 (1965)	Formed in 1964 by merger of eight small railway workers' unions
Union des Syndicates Croyants du Cameroun (USCC)	E	45—in two groups below	IFCTU, ATUC (see text)	8,500 (1965)	Formed in 1962 by merger of CCSC and UCTC (see text)
1. Fédération Nationale des Travailleurs des Travaux Publics et Bâtiments et Industries Annexes au Cameroun (FNTTB)	E	n.a.	None	n.a.	Formed 1966
2. Fédération Nationale des Enseignants Privés au Cameroun (FNEPCAM)	E	n.a.	None	3,000 (1965)	
West Cameroon Trade Union Congress (WCTUC)	W	8 (below)	Assumed ICFTU affiliations, 1962	20,000 (1965)	Formed in 1962 by merger of seven trade unions (see text)

Table 6 (continued)

Name and type, by function	State	Affiliates	External connections	Membership claimed (last available figures)	Remarks
1. National Union of Bank Employees	W	None	None	n.a.	Formed 1963 by merger of 3 bank employees' unions
2. Industrial Union of Commercial, Clerical and Allied Workers	W	None	ITS–International Federation of Commercial, Clerical and Technical Employees	1,000 (1964)	
3. Cameroon Development Corporation Workers' Union (CDCWU)	W	None	ITS–International Federation of Plantation, Agricultural and Allied Workers (IFPAAW)	10,000 (1965)	Registered 1947; membership claimed in 1958 was 10,700
4. Cameroon Union of Plantation, Industrial and Agricultural Workers	W	None	None	820 (1966)	Based in Bamenda

Organization					
5. Likomba Plantation Workers' Union	W	None	ITS–IFPAAW	800 (1962)	
6. Post and Telegraph Workers Union	W	None	ITS–IFPAAW	800 (1962)	Registered 1950
7. Cameroon Public Employees' Union	W	None	None	3,000 (1966)	Formed 1965
8. Teachers' Union	W	None	ITS–International Federation of Free Teachers' Unions	3,000 (1965)	
Cameroonian Nurses Association	W	None	ITS–Public Services International	300 (1964)	Not affiliated with any of the three federations (A, B, C)
AGRICULTURAL ORGANIZATIONS					
Cooperative Union of Bakweri Farmers	W	14	Export handled through Cameroon Development Corporation	2,000 (1964)	Organized by E. M. L. Endeley in 1951–52 on a tribal basis; principally a marketing group

Table 6 (continued)

Name and type, by function	State	Affiliates	External connections	Membership claimed (last available figures)	Remarks
Other cooperatives in West (by type)	W		None		Capitalized at £489,919 with a turnover for 1959 of £3,091,578; many organized on a tribal basis
Thrift and credit		191		ca. 16,000 (1965)	
Thrift and loan		6		183	
		5		215	
Produce and marketing		165		ca. 15,000	
Secondaries		15		470	
Action Paysanne	E	ca. 200	Loosely allied with Cameroon National Union party	2,000–5,000 (1966)	Quasi-political organization, formed 1957 principally to protect interests of Bulu and Fang farmer groups; Gaston Medou, president, was Eastern Assembly deputy; most important are 4 coffee-producing and marketing co-ops of Bamiléké (8,000) and Bamun (3,000) planters
Chambre d'Agriculture, de l'Elevage et des Forêts du Cameroun	E	54	None	n.a.	Includes agricultural syndicates for coffee planters (28 exporters), timber producers (16 firms), and rubber planters (2 firms)

Cooperatives in East (by type)	E	ca. 1,500	None	10,000–
Consumers		5		15,000 (1966)
Secondaries		4		
Produce and marketing		65		
Workers		4		
Mutual credit		ca. 1,300		
Employees		2		
Other		120		

YOUTH AND CHILDREN'S GROUPS

Boy Scouts	W		International Boy Scouts	ca. 2,500 (1965)
Girl Scouts	W		International Girl Guides	ca. 1,000 (1965)
Union des Etudiants Kamerunais (National Union of Kamerun Students)	E-W	59	Informal ties with UPC	n.a.	Most Cameroon students studying abroad
Boys' Brigades	W	4	Cameroon Baptist Convention	n.a.

PROFESSIONAL ORGANIZATIONS

National Order of Physicians	E-W	None		15 (1964)
National Order of Pharmacists	E-W	None	Group of African Pharmacists	27 (1963)
National Order of Attorneys	E	None		n.a.

Table 6 (continued)

Name and type, by function	State	Affiliates	External connections	Membership claimed (last available figures)	Remarks
COMMERCIAL AND INDUSTRIAL GROUPS					
Syndicats des Industriels du Cameroun	E	67	Industrial firms	n.a.	Founded in 1950; represents the principal manufacturing and processing firms in Cameroon
Chamber of Commerce, Industry and Mines of Cameroon	E	156	Commercial and industrial firms, syndicates, unions, etc.; a public corporation	n.a.	

* In October 1969, the three principal trade union organizations (the FSC, USCC, and WCTUC) agreed to form a single body, the Workers' Union of Cameroon (UTC—in French, Union des Travailleurs Camerounais). The new union left the older structures virtually intact, however.

† n.a. = not available.

federations (the WCTUC and two from the East) agreed to form a single body, the Union des Travailleurs Camerounais (UTC—in English, the Workers' Union of Cameroon). The new organization represented the result of efforts by President Ahidjo and the ruling Cameroon National Union party to bring all the trade unions under its wing. As of April 1971, however, the three component federations continued to operate much as they had before the merger, save that they and their member unions were now operating under closer official scrutiny than before.

Until 1969, all trade unions in East Cameroon were grouped into two federations, the Fédération des Syndicats du Cameroun (FSC) and the Union des Syndicats Croyants du Cameroun (USCC) (see Table 6). The FSC was created on January 23, 1963, in Yaoundé, as the culmination of a long series of efforts to unify the trade-union movement. The FSC represents perhaps 87 per cent of all East Cameroon trade-union members; the 1963 merger brought together the Union des Syndicats Libres du Cameroun (USLC), the Union Générale des Travailleurs du Cameroun (UGTC), the Confédération Générale Camerounaise du Travail (CGCT), the Union des Syndicats Autonomes Camerounais (USAC), and some independent unions. The USAC, UGTC, and CGCT were considered the most radical of the Cameroon's trade unions; the CGCT had at one time been the local branch of the Communist-dominated French Confédération Générale du Travail, and the UGTC and the CGCT had had close liaison with both the "militant" pan-African Union Générale des Travailleurs d'Afrique Noire (UGTAN) and the Communist World Federation of Trade Unions (WFTU). The USLC was affiliated with the ICFTU. The whole Fédération now has nominal liaison with the ICFTU and is affiliated with the continent-wide African Trade Union Confederation (ATUC), links which indicate the extent to which most of the trade-union leaders have in fact moved from previously leftist positions. The other federation, the USCC, which claimed about 8,500 members in 1965, was formed in 1962 by the merger of two Christian trade unions, the Confédération Camerounaise des Syndicats Croyants (CCSC) and the Union Camerounaise des Travailleurs Croyants (UCTC). The USCC is affiliated with the ATUC, and the Pan-African Union of Believing Workers, the regional branch of the International Federation of Christian Trade Unions (IFCTU).

Table 6 also gives an indication of the range of modern agricultural organizations found in the Federal Republic. In both states the cooperative movement has flourished and now organizes a significant number of the smaller plantations on both sides of the frontier. Many of these cooperatives are organized along ethnic lines, principally because of the convenience of dealing with people of the same background and because the plantations, more often than not, tend to be located within the traditional geographic boundaries of the tribe to which their owners belong. In West Cameroun, most cooperatives profess to be nonpolitical and to have little to do with the main political parties. This is not entirely true. The Bakweri cooperatives, for one, were intimately linked to Dr. Endeley and the CPNC.

In East Cameroon, the picture is less clear. Although figures are not available, it is reported that many cooperatives have had working liaisons with various political parties. A loose organization, the Union Bamiléké, that grouped Bamiléké peasants and planters and included some cooperatives, was organized in 1948 for solidary, security, and political reasons. The Union Bamiléké was dissolved in 1961, and its members formally committed themselves to support the Union Camerounaise. A similar grouping of Bulu and Fang farmers, the Action Paysanne, organized originally to advance the agricultural interests of its members, became a political party and in 1956 elected nine deputies to the French Cameroun Legislative Assembly.

These and a large number of other organizations play various roles in Cameroonian society. They may act as organizational bases and spokesmen for economic and social interests. They often provide psychological reinforcement for individuals of the same ethnic, social, and economic status or occupational category. Finally, as seen above, to gain their ends they not infrequently become actively engaged in politics or ally themselves with political parties. According to the reasons for their existence, they may perform any or all these roles; indeed, in the context of the Cameroon's changing internal situation, it is often difficult to categorize them at all. A case in point is the Action Paysanne (see Table 6), which is at once an interest group representing a well-defined sector of farmers and planters, a social organization that sponsors local and regional business meetings and more festive gatherings, and an adjunct to a political party, the Union Camerounaise.

Organizations of the type discussed here are often described in terms of the extent to which they establish and maintain ties with particular tribal or ethnic groups. It is rather difficult, in both Cameroon states, to dissociate these bodies from tribal or ethnic connections, simply because many use ethnic identification as the submerged base on which organization, programs, and goals are built. The distinction between tribal and nontribal ties becomes easily blurred since an organization's tribal identification very often simply represents a convenient framework for organization and may facilitate communication within the group. For example, although a group of Bamiléké planters may organize a producers' cooperative, their primary concern is agricultural production, and the Bamiléké connection is a convenience rather than the reason for the organization. It makes more sense, then, to discuss these groups according to the interests they represent or the activity in which they engage and to consider tribal affiliation, when it exists, as a factor which becomes important only to the degree that the organization stresses it. This is not to deny that there are many groups which function as modern or traditional organs of specific ethnic groups. The latter, however, usually take on importance if they become active participants in the political arena. They are more appropriately discussed under the heading "Political Dynamics" (see p. 93). The groups categorized in Table 6, then, are modern groups to which the question of tribal or ethnic identification either is irrelevant or, if such identification exists, is secondary to the purposes of the organizations.

RELIGION

In neither of the Cameroon states is there an official religion. Since the beginning of colonial activity in Cameroun, various Christian missions have been proselytizing in the territory. The result of their activities has been that roughly 27 per cent of the population in West Cameroon and 35 per cent of that of East Cameroon have been Christianized. Muslim influences have operated for centuries in the Cameroon north, but it was not until the beginning of the nineteenth century and the jihad of Usuman Dan Fodio that much of the Cameroonian reaches of the Chad plain and the Adamawa Plateau was Islamized. Two consequences of Muslim activity in the north are that Christian mission work has been more or less limited to the area south of the Adamawa Plateau and that the overwhelming number of Cameroon Christians are found in that region. It is estimated that there are about 600,000 Muslims in East Cameroon, most of them residing north of the inland forest plateau. Proselytizing on the part of both Christian missionaries and Muslim teachers still goes on, much of it directed at the large numbers of animist peoples who constitute about 45 per cent of the population in the East and about 65 per cent in West Cameroon.

The Christian missions, among the first Westernizing influences in Cameroon, have tended to dominate the educational effort in the two states and continue to provide a variety of medical and social services such as hospitals, leprosaria, dispensaries, maternity centers, orphanages, and the like. In West Cameroon, particularly, nearly all primary and secondary schools are run by them. In East Cameroon 17 of the 34 hospitals and 69 of the 395 infirmaries and dispensaries are operated by religious voluntary agencies. In West Cameroon the voluntary agencies operate 2 of the 24 hospitals, all the maternity centers, and both leprosaria. In both states the social service institutions—

hospitals, schools, and so on—that are run by the voluntary agencies operate under government supervision and benefit from partial public subsidy.

Education [17]

Unification has markedly affected the once separate educational systems of the two states. West Cameroon came to unification with a system based on British matriculation and grading patterns, East Cameroon with one based upon French models. Integration of the two systems, a natural consequence of federal union, came slowly, but by 1965 the outlines of a national system were visible. To begin with, under the federal constitution, secondary, technical, and higher education are the responsibility of the federal government, while preschool and primary education remains under state jurisdiction. The latter reservation was deemed necessary to meet the special problems faced at the local level, including the continuing use of vernacular languages at the lowest primary levels. The language problem has been one of the most vexing faced by Cameroon's educational reformers. It is official policy that French be taught in all schools above the primary level in West Cameroon, and that English be similarly taught above the

[17] Extended discussion of education in Cameroon may be found in the following: Victor T. Le Vine and Henri M'Ballah, "[Education in the] Federal Republic of Cameroon," in Helen Kitchen, ed., *The Educated African* (New York: Praeger, 1962), pp. 519–532; Victor T. Le Vine, *The Cameroons from Mandate to Independence,* pp. 304–306; Hugon, *op. cit.,* pp. 295–302; E. A. Podesta, *Education and Manpower,* Vol. VII of *The Economic Potential of West Cameroon* (Menlo Park, Calif.: Stanford Research Institute, 1965); Martena Sasnet and Inez Sepmeyer, *Educational Systems of Africa* (Berkeley: University of California Press, 1966), "Cameroon," pp. 626–627.

primary grades in East Cameroon. The ultimate aim, of course, is to make all education truly bilingual. Considerable strides have been taken toward this goal, but a lack of trained bilingual personnel and some local resistance has slowed progress in this area, and most instruction in West Cameroon continues to be in English, that in East Cameroon, in French.[18] At least one measure of the pace at which bilingualism can realistically be achieved is the fact that the only school in West Cameroon in which all instructors are bilingual is the Federal Bilingual Grammar (Secondary) School at Man 'o War Bay, Victoria, which opened in 1963. The *lycée* at Buea, which offers the Certificate of Primary Studies (BEPC) and an upper secondary course in arts, is expected to be fully staffed by bilingual personnel soon.

On other fronts, however, notable progress has been made toward establishing a truly integrated school system for the whole country. In 1965, for example, the second stage of the so-called structural harmonization of primary education took place in West Cameroon with the inauguration of a six-year primary cycle.[19] Before "harmonization," the standard West cycle had been eight years; that of the East, six. By 1967, the harmonization of secondary syllabuses for languages, mathematics, history, and geography had achieved marked progress in both states. Also notable is the fact that between 1960 and 1966 school at-

[18] For further comment on this matter, see H. O. H. Vernon-Jackson, *Language, Schools and Government in Cameroon* (New York: Columbia University, Teachers College Press, 1967).

[19] Details of the plan to integrate the two systems are contained in Ministry of Education and Social Welfare, West Cameroon, *West Cameroon Education Policy* (Buea: The Ministry, 1963).

tendance in the elementary grades virtually doubled; during the same period, attendance in secondary schools almost trebled, and, what is more, five institutions of higher education were inaugurated where none had existed before 1960. In 1968, Cameroon had a school-attendance rate of 67 per cent, one of the highest in French-speaking Africa; in the southern areas of the country, the rate is almost 100 per cent. Harmonization has also involved attempts to equalize the lengths of courses, and to synchronize the school year and school holidays in both states.

The basic structural features of the Cameroon's educational system are relatively easy to describe. In sum, the system provides six years' elementary training, with appropriate certification at the end, followed by alternative plans for secondary education, depending on placement in examinations, occupational preferences, or other factors. West Cameroon offers a full five-year secondary school course with the possibility of entrance to higher educational institutions, a four-year terminal technical college program, and a three- or five-year teacher training course. East Cameroon's secondary system is more complex. Those who finish primary school may, upon due certification, enter the complete seven-year secondary program (*lycée*) leading to the *baccalauréat*. Here, the student may elect either the "classical" or "modern languages" program. Alternatively, primary-school finishers who cannot or do not want to enter the *lycée* may choose the seven-year *lycée technique* or the so-called five-year short-cycle technical college program. Also available is a four-year technical training school, a group of two-year programs stressing artisan, rural, and homemaking skills, or a terminal two-year "practical" training course (*section pratique de fin d'études*). Higher education—available to those completing one of the long secondary courses—includes, in West Cameroon, the College of Arts, Science and Technology, and in East Cameroon, the Cameroon Federal University, the Cameroon School of Administration, and four other institutions (see Table 7). The Federal University, set up in 1962, deserves further mention, if only for its attempt to create a genuine bilingual institution of higher learning. For the first five years of its existence, the University was housed in temporary quarters; in 1967 and 1970 it moved into two new sets of buildings, constructed mainly with financing from the French Aid and Cooperation Fund (in the amount of about $6 million). Completed buildings now include faculties of law, science, and letters, administration buildings, housing for students and teachers, and a Center for African Research. A medical school is under construction. About 10 per cent of the 2,000 students are English-speaking from West Cameroon, and efforts are being made to find bilingual staff to accomodate them. As of April 1971, however, the University was still heavily *francophone,* and the French cultural influence seemed nearly overwhelming. Almost all instruction was in French, and the administration of the school lay in the hands of *francophone* Cameroonians and Frenchmen. Nevertheless, the University's administrators and the government are trying to see that it meets the needs of the country and, in a broader sense, of Africa. According to one report: "The introduction of an African orientation to the curricula has . . . been pressed ahead . . . and there are more senior African members of staff, both English and French-speaking, helping it toward the hoped-for position of halfway house between *anglophonie* and *francophonie.*" [20]

[20] "Yaoundé Halfway House," *West Africa,* July 18, 1970, p. 793.

Table 7. Schools and school enrollment in Cameroon
(latest available statistics)

Type of school	No. of schools (1964–65)	Enrollment (1967–68)
West Cameroon		
Primary	686	122,000
Secondary		
General (including 1 *lycée*)	14	3,893
Vocational (technical and teacher training)	13	3,213
College of Arts and Sciences, Bambui	1	183
Technical College, Ombe	1	287
East Cameroon		
Primary	3,380	643,449
Secondary		
General (including 10 *lycées*)	108	33,448
Technical	47	9,685
Teacher training	n.a.*	1,383
Higher		
Cameroon Federal University and Cameroon School of Administration		2,196 †
Higher Federal School of Agriculture		56
Ecole Normale Supérieure		250
Ecole Camerounaise d'Administration et de Magistrature		n.a.
Ecole Interarmes Militaire		60
Students abroad		
Combined, East and West Cameroon		(1966–67) 1,116 ‡

* n.a. = not available.

† The UNESCO *Yearbook* reported that this represented an increase of 392 (21.7%) over the previous year.

‡ 503 on scholarships.

Sources: Data on West Cameroon drawn from E. A. Podesta, *Education and Manpower,* Vol. VII of *The Economic Potential of West Cameroon* (Menlo Park: Stanford Research Institute, 1965). Data on East Cameroon drawn from bulletins of East Cameroon Secretariat of State for Education; UNESCO, *International Yearbook of Education,* Vol. XXX (Paris: UNESCO, 1968); and *UNESCO Statistical Yearbook, 1968* (Paris: UNESCO, 1968).

Among the pressing problems confronting Cameroon's educational system, bilingualism aside, are a lack of qualified teaching personnel and an abnormally high dropout rate. Philippe Hugon summarizes the latter situation: "Cameroon, together with Gabon, has one of the lowest education production rates in all of black Africa. For every 1,000 pupils enrolled in the first [primary] grade, only 398 finish the sixth [terminal] grade, and of those, only 100 actually receive the C.E.P.E. [elementary certificate— Certificat d'Etudes Primaires Elémentaires]." [21] Hugon calls this situation *un grand gaspillage,* a massive squandering of human and physical resources, primarily a result of the fact, as he sees it, that the present system is ill-adapted to needs of a developing country such as Cameroon. He has probably overstated the case, but the fact remains that only very few emerge from the narrow end of the primary, much less the secondary, funnel. Nevertheless, Cameroon's educational system is being adapted, however slowly, to the realities of unification and developmental needs of the country.

Press and Communications Media

As is the case in many African states, the press, while not altogether controlled, is officially restrained, a federal "Freedom of the Press" statute (1966) to the contrary notwithstanding.

Cameroon's only daily, *La Presse du Cameroun,* is published in Douala. Its circulation is confined almost exclusively to the East. The *Presse* is editorially apolitical, is owned by the Paris-Soir chain (which also publishes dailies in Dakar, Abidjan, and elsewhere), and reports local and international news without comment. It is, however, supervised by the government, which approves political notices, letters to the editor, and announcements of a

[21] Hugon, *op. cit.,* p. 296; translation is mine.

political nature. It steers clear of controversy and follows official guidance about matters the government wishes to play down or suppress.

There is one other private newspaper, *L'Effort camerounais,* published weekly by the Paulist Fathers in Yaoundé. *L'Effort* follows a relatively liberal line editorially and is often critical of the government. Within the past few years, a number of issues have been confiscated, including one in April 1962 which reported the death of twenty-five government prisoners in a train on its way to Yaoundé, a story the government very much wanted suppressed. The issue was seized and its editor, a French priest by the name of Fertin, summarily deported. *La Semaine camerounaise,* which came into existence in 1965, and ceased publication in 1970, followed the format of *L'Effort,* providing a mixture of commentary on national and international events, official news and texts, coverage of important local and national events, plus a good deal of material of a religious, in this case Protestant, nature. The paper did not appear to have a coherent editorial policy, save that it was less inclined to oppose official policy overtly, and wrapped its criticisms in the euphemisms of "constructive questions." Three government papers in the East are more or less permanent: one is *L'Unité,* the official weekly organ of the Union Camerounaise, the government party; the second is the daily broadsheets of the Agence Camerounaise de Press consisting mainly of teletype output, and the third is *Le Bamiléké,* published under governmental auspices in the Bamiléké area.

In West Cameroon, the first newspapers of any consequence appeared in 1960 in Victoria. One, the weekly *Cameroons Champion,* which reflected the views of the opposition Cameroons Peoples' National Convention of Dr. Endeley, ceased publication in 1962. Its demise followed the death of its founder, Peter Motomby-Woleta; there are indications that official pressures may have helped the collapse of the paper. The other paper, also a weekly, the *Kamerun Times* (after 1961, *Cameroon Times*), spoke for the West Cameroon government. It ceased publication in April 1968, for what were claimed to be "financial reasons," but resumed publishing in 1969 under new management. Between 1966 and 1969, a number of local newspapers sprang up in West Cameroon, such as the *Cameroon Mirror, Cameroon Spokesman, Cameroon Telegraph, Cameroon Outlook,* and *Cameroon Chronicle.* Others, like *Iroko* and *Cameroon Star* had only a few issues. Some of these papers spoke for the partially-submerged opposition, and they tended to have their lives cut short by official action: *Iroko,* for example, was banned in 1966 for "dissemination of false news" (i.e., criticism of the government). A few magazines, such as *Fako* and the *Cameroon Flash,* appeared briefly and then folded. In 1970, the West Cameroon newspapers (published two or three times a week) were the *Cameroon Times, Cameroon Outlook, Cameroon Workman,* and *Cameroon Telegraph.* Circulation is limited; only the *Times* reaches 5,000 readers and the rest claim a circulation of between 1,500 and 4,300.

A number of other "newspapers" appear from time to time in East Cameroon, most of them mirroring the views of opposition groups. The UPC currently has no official voice, but until recently some of its militants issued various newssheets in printed or mimeographed form. These were devoted principally to violent denunciation of the government and its policies. The UPC sheets, under such titles as *Abolégé, L'Etoile, Le Crabe noir, La Voix du peuple,* and so on, were usually seized after a few issues but subsequently reappeared under different mastheads. The Démocrates issued an irregular paper, *Le Démocrate,* which, however, was little read and appeared so infrequently as to be of little importance.

Radio is wholly a government-controlled enterprise. The Radiodiffusion Camerounaise broadcasts from Yaoundé, Douala, and Garoua, with transmitters at Ngaoundéré, and, recently, Buea. Until unification, West Cameroon had a recording studio affiliated with the Nigerian Broadcasting Corporation. After unification, the West state began to transmit broadcasts from Douala, and finally, in 1967, began operating its own broadcasting facilities in Buea. In 1968, the Soviet Union agreed to construct a 100-kilowatt station at Yaoundé.

CHAPTER 3

The Political Process

Formal Structure

The formal structure of the Cameroon Federal Republic is defined by the constitution which became effective on October 1, 1961. This date also marked the termination of the British Southern Cameroons trusteeship and the end of the Cameroun Republic born on January 1, 1960. It is of some interest that the constitution of 1960 had created a republic that, with some minor adaptations to the local situation, was modeled on the Gaullist constitution of the Fifth Republic. The resemblance was evident not only in the wording of the document but in the nature of the organs created by it, especially in the powers and prerogatives of the President. The 1961 constitution, however, owed every little to its predecessor. The document which emerged from the series of Cameroun-Cameroons conferences in the spring and summer of 1961 was a curious mixture of presidential and parliamentary governmental forms, a mélange bearing the superficial imprint of a series of political compromises between the respective positions of Ahidjo and Foncha, but, in fact, reflecting more eastern wishes than western hopes. Essentially, Foncha and his colleagues had three objectives in mind during the negotiations: (1) to create a set of federal institutions and delimit federal and state jurisdictions; (2) to preserve virtually intact the local autonomy hitherto enjoyed by the two states; and (3) to maintain as long as possible the political status quo in both Cameroons.[1] As things turned out, the easterners shared only the first objective; the final product merely gave the west a short breathing space until most of its important powers were absorbed by the federal government.

FEDERAL DIVISIONS

Article 1, among other things, designates the former British Southern Cameroons and the Republic of Cameroun as West and East Cameroon, respectively. Until the United Nations ratified the results of the February 1961 plebiscite in the British Northern Cameroons, both Foncha and Ahidjo officially hoped that the Northern Cameroons would become the third component of the federation.

[1] I discussed the circumstances surrounding the drafting of the 1961 Constitution in "The New Cameroon Federation," *Africa Report*, VI, No. 11 (Dec. 1961), 7, 8, 10, and in "Unifying the Cameroons," *West Africa*, July 15, 1961, pp. 774–775. For a constitutional analysis of the federal constitution, see the two articles by P. F. Gonidec, "Les institutions politiques de la République Fédérale du Cameroun," *Civilisations*, XI, No. 4 (1961), 370–395, and XII No. 1 (1962), 13–26. Willard Johnson, who was in Cameroon during the early years of unification, discusses the new constitution in *The Cameroon Federation: Political Integration in a Fragmentary Society* (Princeton, N.J.: Princeton University Press, 1970), pp. 200–232, and "The Cameroon Federation: Political Union Between English-speaking and French-speaking Africa," in William H. Lewis, ed., *French-speaking Africa: The Search for Identity* (New York: Walker, 1965), pp. 205–360. Probably the most detailed analysis of the Cameroon federal system, as seen from a legal standpoint, is by H. N. A. Enonchong, *Cameroon Constitutional Law* (Yaoundé: Centre d'Edition et de Production de Manuels et d'Auxiliaires de l'Enseignement, 1967).

Articles 4 through 37 of the constitution describe the organization and competence of the federal government and its various organs. Federal authority, according to Article 4, is exercised by the President of the Federal Republic and the National Federal Assembly. The President, assisted by a Vice-President, is at once head of state and the chief of the federal government. Both President and Vice-President serve five-year terms following their election—from a single state—by direct, secret, and universal suffrage (Articles 8–10). A list of so called "Transitional and Special Dispositions" (Articles 48–60), appended to the main body of the document, stipulate that until the tenure of the incumbent President of the Cameroun Republic expires, he and the incumbent Prime Minister of the Southern Cameroons are to serve respectively as President and Vice-President of the Federal Republic. The effect of this dispensation was to guarantee Ahidjo and Foncha the top federal executive positions until May 5, 1965, when the former's presidential mandate under the 1960 constitution ended. Both were re-elected for another five-year term in 1965.

The federal President selects the members of a federal government "from among the nationals of each of the Federated states." Although the constitution is silent on the subject of a division of ministries between the two states, it is nonetheless clear that both states will be represented in the federal cabinet. The sixteen-man cabinet named on October 20, 1961, included five West Cameroonians, one as a full minister (S. Tandeng Muna, Minister of Transport, Mines, Posts, and Telecommunications), three as deputy ministers (A. N. Jua, Public Health; E. Egbe Tabi, Justice; and Nzo Ekhah Nghaky, Foreign Affairs), and one undersecretary of state (Simon Nji, Production). That ratio appears to have changed in favor of the East; though the federal cabinet reshuffle of August 1968 resulted in five "West" to twelve "East" ministries, the cabinets of 1970 and 1971 included only three "West" to nineteen "East" ministers. There is no provision that federal ministers be members of the Federal Assembly, and, in fact, at least three of the eastern group of federal ministers of 1961 were not parliamentarians (Jean-Faustin Betayéné, Minister of Foreign Affairs; Charles Onana Awana, Minister Delegate to the Presidency for Finance and the Plan; and Dr. Simon Tchoungui, Minister of Public Health).

In addition to the usual executive functions, powers, and prerogatives, the federal President is given several other special powers by the constitution. He appoints the prime ministers and cabinets of the states.[2] He must be "consulted" by the governments of the two states when those governments take measures which may "affect the life of the Federation" (Article 13). In practice, according to some authorities, this could give the President the power to intervene if either state government does anything which might adversely affect the nation as a whole. Article 13 is reinforced by Article 14, which gives the President the right to seek an advisory opinion from the Federal

[2] President Ahidjo has exercised this power five times since 1961: three times to name a West prime minister (A. N. Jua, on May 12, 1965; S. T. Muna, to succeed Jua, on Jan. 11, 1968; and Muna, to succeed himself, on May 15, 1970) and twice to name a premier for East Cameroon (Dr. Simon-Pierre Tchoungui, in 1965; and again, to succeed himself, on June 12, 1970).

Court of Justice if state legislation appears to contravene the federal constitution or a federal law. Further, in wording almost exactly like that employed by the celebrated Article 16 of the constitution of the Fifth French Republic, the President may "in case of grave peril threatening the integrity of the territory, the life, independence, or institutions of the nation" proclaim a state of emergency by decree and then "take all measures he judges necessary." In so doing, he is limited only by the necessity of "consulting" with the prime ministers of the states and by the presence of the Federal Assembly, which may meet for the duration of emergency.[3] In all, the constitution creates a hybrid President who combines attributes of a British-style governor-general, a Fifth Republic president, and an American chief executive. This new type of presidency does not appear to have parallels in present or past constitutional practice.

Although there is no direct evidence to substantiate it, it has been suggested that this type of regime was tailor-made to suit the needs and demands of President Ahidjo. The legislative committee of the Cameroon National Assembly which reported out the draft of the new constitution defended the portions of the document relating to the presidency by a reference to France and the virtues of what is termed "Presidential democracy," a concept to which Ahidjo is known to be attached:

The aim of the advocates of this constitutional revision was . . . to consolidate the authority of the State, avoiding the creation of a machinery of state that would be too com-

---

[3] In French constitutional practice "consultation" does not necessarily imply that advice tendered need be heeded. All that is required is formal discussion.

plex or cumbersome, whose slowness could prevent it from responding to the increasingly urgent needs of modern life. . . .

The presidential regime is manifestly [that regime] which can best handle these imperatives and which most properly confers upon the executive [power] the qualities of performance that one can expect of it.

One may note, moreover, that the presidential system is on the increase thoroughout the world and that all the democracies use it more and more frequently. The change in the parliamentary system provided, for example, by the Fifth French Republic, is evidence of a vigorous—though incomplete—orientation toward presidential democracy.[4]

If it is assumed that constitutional forms have some influence on political events, then there is little question that the definition of the powers of the Cameroon federal President reinforced, rather than hindered, Ahidjo's attempt to create a one-party state.

The federal Vice-President has no fixed functions. He assists the President, who may delegate responsibilities to him by decree. However, in the event the Presidency becomes vacant, "for any reason whatsoever" (Article 10), the Vice-President assumes the Presidency until the next presidential elections. Mr. Foncha's tenure in that office was more honorific than substantive. In fact, in May 1965, Foncha had to resign his position as Prime Minister of West Cameroon, which post he had held concurrently with his Vice-Presidency. It is perhaps surprising that Foncha

[4] Commission des Lois Constitutionnelles, de la Justice, et de la Législation, de l'Administration Générale de la République, et des Forces Armées, "Rapport," cited in *La Presse du Cameroun* (Douala), Aug. 17, 1961, p. 3. The translation is mine.

kept both jobs for so long in the face of an explicit constitutional prohibition ("The offices of President and Vice-President . . . shall be incompatible with any other office" —Article 9), but it is understandable that Foncha was reluctant to give up what real formal power was left him after unification. It should be added that under the changed political conditions of 1970—the choice of West Cameroon Prime Minister S. T. Muna as Ahidjo's vice-presidential running mate in the March 1970 presidential elections—the Constitution was amended (after the elections) to permit Muna to be reappointed as Western Prime Minister (Law No. 70/LF/1 of May 4, 1970).

The Federal Assembly is elected for five years by direct, secret, and universal suffrage in each state on the basis of one deputy for each 80,000 inhabitants (Article 16). The "Transitional Dispositions" (Articles 53, 54) postponed federal elections until at least April 1964; until that date the two legislatures were to select the members of the Federal Assembly from their numbers according to the 1:80,000 ratio fixed by Article 16. The "Transitional and Special Dispositions" do not specifically fix either the number of deputies in the Federal Assembly or the division of seats between the states; this is done indirectly by stating that for the purposes of the constitution at the time of its promulgation East Cameroon has 3,200,000 and West Cameroon has 800,000 inhabitants (Article 60). The first Federal Assembly selected in April 1961 comprised forty deputies from the East and ten from the West. The official population figures on which the distribution of seats is based do not correspond to any actual enumeration of population since no full census has even been conducted in Cameroon. They may, however, be modified by a federal law if a national census is taken. The federal elections were in fact held in 1964, as they were in 1970; the 40:10 East-West ratio was maintained in both instances. An amendment to the Constitution adopted in November 1969 permits the Federal Assembly, on the initiative of the President, to extend or shorten its mandate (Law No. 69/LF/14 of November 10, 1969).

The Federal Assembly meets annually in two sessions, one of which must be devoted to the budget and neither of which is to exceed thirty days' duration. Special sessions, called by either the President or by request of two-thirds of the Assembly, may not exceed fifteen days (Article 19). Voting is by simple majority of all deputies (Article 17) except in the case of the novel procedures described by Article 18 which provide for a curious system of regional checks on national action:

Before a law is promulgated, the President of the Federal Republic may request a second reading thereof, either on his own motion or at the request of either of the Prime Ministers of the Federated States. On second reading, the law shall be adopted *only if the majority* specified in the preceding article *comprises a majority of the votes of the deputies of each of the Federated States.* (Article 18, italics added.)

This provision, in effect, creates a type of concurrent majority voting system whose use could prevent the passage of any federal legislation or constitutional amendment (Article 47) to which either state objected. Operationally the device could have even more serious consequences. If the 1971 membership of the Federal Assembly is used as an example, the majority envisaged by Article 18 would have to include 6 of the 10 West Cameroon deputies, plus

21 from the eastern state. Ultimately, any 20 easterners (even more significantly) any 5 westerners could block any legislation. Assuming agreement by the West Cameroon government (since all members are instructed on their vote) the device amounts to giving 10 per cent of the members of the Federal Assembly a permanent veto over its deliberations. In view of the political circumstances surrounding the drafting of the constitution, one suspects that Article 18 was included as one of several measures designed to guarantee Prime Minister Foncha a maximum of local autonomy coupled with a minimum of federal interference. Since the article has never been invoked, it may well have been that the guarantee was symbolic, not real.[5]

The constitution completes the executive-legislative-judicial triad by creating two exclusively federal courts: one, the Federal Court of Justice (Articles 33, 34), as the highest court in the judicial system, and the other, the High Court of Justice (Article 36), as a special court to try cases of high treason or conspiracy against the state or to judge instances of malfeasance by the President, the Vice-President, the federal ministers, the prime ministers, and the

[5] A preplebiscite communiqué defining the general "Constitutional Position of the Southern Cameroons in the Event of It Electing to Become Part of the Republic of Cameroun," signed by both Foncha and Ahidjo on Oct. 13, 1960, presaged this article: "Certain federal laws will only be enacted in such a way that no measures contrary to the interest of one State will be imposed upon it by the majority (system of second reading with qualified majority)." See *The Two Alternatives*, Printed by Authority [of the Commissioner of the United Kingdom in the Southern Cameroons] (Buea, Dec. 1960), p. 14. Enonchong, *op. cit.*, p. 112, makes an analysis similar to my own; he notes, however, that this device, as of 1967, had not yet been used. It was not used in 1968, 1969, or 1970, either.

ministers of the states. The Federal Court of Justice is the final court of appeals for federal cases arising in the state courts; it adjudicates disputes between the states or between a state and the federal government, has jurisdiction over cases involving abuse of administrative discretion by federal authorities, and decides on the constitutionality of state statutes and (upon application of Article 14, for example) of legislation pending before the Federal Assembly. In the latter cases, the size of the Court is doubled by adding to it members drawn from a panel of individuals annually selected by the President "by reason of their competence or experience" (Article 34).

Finally, the constitution creates a Federal Economic and Social Council and, by implication (see below), a Federal Council of the Magistracy, plus a rather shadowy Federal Coordinating Committee. The Economic and Social Council, whose functions are not spelled out in the constitution, was set up in 1963 as a consultative body incorporating representatives of industry, management, labor, agriculture, and so on. Its model was undoubtedly the East Cameroon's Economic and Social Council, itself a vague and almost purely honorific body. The Council of the Magistracy was not specifically created by the constitution but according to Article 32 is to assist the President in the administration of the judicial system, particularly in the selection of judges and in matters of discipline. It was in fact set up in 1962. The Federal Coordinating Committee, mentioned in two articles (7 and 13), is an *ad hoc* body created by the President to deal with possible conflicts of state-federal jurisdiction or authority in areas where, in the language of the constitution, the "states may temporarily intervene." These areas, as defined by Article

6, include all jurisdictions which fall within federal competence only after an undefined "transition period." The Coordinating Committee must also be consulted under the circumstances foreseen in Article 13.

FEDERAL JURISDICTIONS

Superficially, the scope of federal power appears quite broad. Two lists are provided by the constitution, one enumerating federal jurisdictions in which federal organs may operate "immediately" (Article 5) and the other listing areas which will become subject to federal authority after the "transition period" (Article 6). The first list includes such matters as nationality, national defense, foreign affairs, currency and money, federal administration, and the like. The second list includes secondary education, the "regime of public liberties," local judicial organization and administration, land law, and labor regulation—areas originally, but by and large no longer, under state control. The areas defined in Article 6 were expected eventually to become federal concerns but, according to one official commentary published in 1961, "There is less urgency about having them fall under federal competence, and besides, they pose extremely delicate problems of adaptation . . . [and] the Federated States may either legislate or direct appropriate administrative services in these areas until the Federal authorities step in." [6] As it turned out, the federal authorities "stepped in" in the persons of federal administrators and through state officials included (personally, and by function) within the federal structure. As a result, the process of "adaptation" was speeded up,

[6] Commission des Lois Constitutionnelles, . . . , *op. cit.*, p. 4; translation is mine.

so that by 1963 most areas listed in Article 6 had fallen under *de facto* federal jurisdiction. It is also intertesting to note that Article 6 refers to one of the two entrenched rights reserved to West Cameroon, the maintenance of the customary law courts. The other entrenched right is mentioned in Article 38, which guarantees—in addition to all rights not enumerated—the maintenance of the West Cameroon House of Chiefs.

THE STATES AND FEDERAL-STATE RELATIONS

The constitution has little to say about the relations between the states and the federal government, save to define the powers of the President in respect to the selection and termination of state governments and in relation to laws passed by the state assemblies. The President designates each state's prime minister, who until 1970, was invested by his state's legislature. A change in the constitution enacted in that year made investiture by the state legislatures unnecessary. Upon the nomination of the prime ministers, the President names and dismisses the members of the state governments. When and if a state government falls—when its legislature refuses confidence or votes a motion of censure—the prime minister concerned must submit his resignation to the President. If a state government and its legislature are in "persistent disagreement," the President may dissolve the legislature on his own initiative or on that of the prime minister involved and then call new elections after two months. The President promulgates all laws passed by the state legislatures; if he disapproves of a state law sent to him for signature, he may invoke Article 18 and call for a second reading or ask the Federal Court of Justice for an advisory opinion regarding the law's constitutionality (Articles 44, 45).

The states are each arrogated all powers not specifically given to the federal government, and all laws pre-existing the constitution and not in conflict with it are permitted to remain in force (Article 46). In the final analysis, this leaves the state legislatures very little to do.

Each state has its own legislature; that in the West is bicameral, composed of the House of Chiefs and the Legislative Assembly, that in the East is the unicameral Legislative Assembly. The constitution fixes five years as the life of the state legislatures and their membership at 37 for the West (excluding the House of Chiefs, whose membership can vary) and 100 for the East. One other stipulation is of interest: state elections are to be held under universal suffrage and representation is to be on the basis of "each administrative unit [represented] proportionally to the number of [its] population." Although it may have been intended, particularly by Foncha, that each state would continue to maintain a considerable degree of local autonomy, what in fact came about was a near monopoly of powers in the hands of the federal government.

Political Dynamics

A "national" Cameroonian political system, in the sense of a recognizable set of political symbols, roles, institutions, personalities, and organizations, was—not unexpectedly—slow to emerge. For one thing, despite the fact that the federal constitution provided for a greater measure of centralization than Foncha had wanted, its Articles 53 and 54 effectively deferred federal electoral activity until 1964, and a set of presidential decrees put off state elections until 1965. The provisions embodied, as it were, a more or less explicit guarantee that the two political systems, united after forty years of separate development, could continue to go their respective ways relatively unhindered until living together became part of the political consciousness of citizens on both sides of the interstate border. The official reason concealed a related but simpler reason: the understandable reluctance of western leaders to allow eastern politicians, with their vastly superior resources, grazing rights in the fertile political fields they had carefully cultivated for their own use. In the final analysis, the West's leaders could only delay the inevitable: that the system as a whole would come to be dominated by the larger of the two states and its internal politics by policies and groups of eastern inspiration. Certainly by the beginning of 1968, when Solomon T. Muna—known as a strong "federal" man—assumed the prime ministership of West Cameroon, that process was already well under way. Given the predilections, experience, and values of President Ahidjo and his closest colleagues, it is not inconceivable that the next steps—albeit in the indeterminate future— may well be in the direction of a unitary state. It is this growth of a "national" system, then, that gives structure to and underlines the dynamics of Cameroonian politics since 1961.[7]

[7] Willard Johnson's book, *The Cameroon Federation: Political Integration in a Fragmentary Society* (Princeton, N.J.: Princeton University Press, 1970) provides the fullest account of the first five years of federation. Edwin Ardener's perceptive "The Nature of the Reunification of Cameroon," in Arthur Hazelwood, ed., *African Integration and Disintegration* (London: Oxford University Press,

WEST CAMEROON POLITICS

Though reunification was widely hailed in both states, it did in fact bring some initial discomfort to West Cameroonians. Ardener has summarized the situation:

The years 1960–3 were marked by the activities of the Federal Gendarmerie whose encampments were established in or near the major centres. The occasional severities of the new forces of security can be attributed to their limited education, and to their experiences in terrorist areas of the East. It had been feared that the West was a haven for bandits. The searching of lorries, the questioning of travellers, and the use of public violence, were a novelty to the West Cameroon population. Complaints finally appeared in the press alleging that even police and officials and their families were not immune from assaults. The situation quickly eased after 1963. It was during this period that East Cameroonian officials began to acquire a genuine respect for the high degree of law and order in the West, and in due course, the public behaviour of the gendarmerie began to approximate that of the unarmed West Cameroon police. To Westerners must go the credit that their attitude to the gendarmerie was kept separate from their attitude to reunification. No political voices were raised in criticism by either the CPNC opposition, then in eclipse, or publicly, by the KNDP government.[8]

The first general elections to West Cameroon Legislative Assembly, which was enlarged to 37 seats (from its earlier

---

1967), pp. 285–337, examines the union from the point of view of West Cameroon. Other than occasional articles in *West Africa, Europe-France-Outremer, Afrique Nouvelle, Jeune Afrique,* and other periodicals, there is little analysis of post-reunification politics in Cameroon.

[8] Ardener, *op. cit.,* pp. 331–332.

26) by the federal constitution, were held on January 7, 1962. Prime Minister Foncha had chosen a good time for the election; to no one's surprise the KNDP, still basking in the warm glow of reunification, won an absolute majority in the Western Assembly. The final allocation of seats gave the KNDP twenty-five; Dr. Endeley's CPNC took ten, the OK one, and one went to an independent who, together with the OK member, immediately declared his support for the government. Endeley himself remained as the salaried leader of the opposition. Two results of the elections deserve mention. First, with the seating of the lone OK member, for the first time in the history of the Southern Cameroons–West Cameroon, all the major parties were represented, if only briefly, in the legislature. Second, the distribution of seats reflected with some accuracy the relative importance and electoral support of the parties.

Between 1962 and 1966 West Cameroon witnessed a complex political ballet in which the principal parties and politicians simultaneously strove to retain their influence in the West and maneuvered to put themselves in the best possible position for the merger of all parties at the national level, a step to which they had committed themselves at the outset. To begin with, the KNDP did not merge with the CPNC, though both stood, ostensibly, by their statements of August 1962, in which they declared their intention of joining a true "national party" of which the UC/KNDP "Unity Group" in the Federal Assembly was the model and precursor. At this point, however, the parties parted company. The CPNC contended that both CPNC and KNDP should be dissolved when the East and West parties finally merged. The KNDP, on the other hand, stated that one must first join the KNDP in order to enter the Union Camerounaise: "By coming into the KNDP one is already joining with the UC to work out a programme for the formation of a National Party through the coordination Committee" (which had been set up between the KNDP and the UC to plan for eventual union).[9] The two parties had, in April 1961, issued a joint statement, reaffirmed in the "truce" of May 11, 1961, wherein both pledged to "forget the past and work together toward the achievement of a happy and prosperous Kamerun country." The truce, if it showed good intentions, did not, however, eliminate the long-standing differences between the KNDP and CPNC leaders. It became apparent in 1962 that the KNDP strategy was to eliminate the CPNC as a possible negotiating party when the parties eventually merged on the national level.

In 1963 it also became obvious that the impending national party merger as well as other considerations had precipitated a rift within the KNDP itself.

At the KNDP National Convention of that year [1963], the choice of the acknowledged deputy and successor-apparent to Mr. Foncha became important, in view of the approach of the date after which the posts of Prime Minister and Vice-President would, under the Constitution, be separated. At the same time the Secretary-Generalship of the party had become vacant. Both posts were contested: the greater by A. N. Jua (the West Cameroon Minister of Finance) and S. T. Muna (federal Minister of Transport and Communications), and the lesser by E. Egbe (federal Deputy Minister of Foreign Affairs). Muna was commonly regarded as a "Federation" man, possi-

[9] I am grateful to Willard Johnson for the partial texts of the KNDP (Aug. 11, 1962) and CPNC (Aug. 10, 1962) press releases.

bly because he was a man of great energy and determination who was genuinely bound up in his ministerial responsibilities, which he saw as the way of bringing to his State those great constructions and public works which he admired in the East. He was respected for his ability by the President. Mr. Jua was believed to be a West Cameroonian first and foremost. This was also probably an overstatement. He had never antagonized any section of the party, and he had a good, even flamboyant, record of political activity when KNDP had been in opposition. He had retained a keen sense for movements in West Cameroon popular feeling, and he had played a large role in maintaining the impetus in favour of reunification in the pre-plebiscite period—Mr. Jua was the party's choice. For the Secretary-Generalship the selection was Nzo Ekah-Nghaky, a member of the new intelligentsia.[10]

The struggle at the KNDP convention, as it turned out, benefited the CPNC by turning the KNDP's attentions inward, easing the pressure on the opposition for an early merger with the KNDP. It also left Muna and Egbe unrepentant; in May 1965, when Foncha finally vacated the West prime ministership, Muna was still very much in contention for the job. Treading carefully, the President went to Buea to sound out all shades of opinion, and finally selected Jua to succeed Foncha. Foncha, angered by the turn of events, on his own authority, turned on Muna, drumming him out of the KNDP, along with Egbe, and six other members of the Assembly who had committed themselves to Muna's cause. Foncha also tried to get Ahidjo to discharge Muna and Egbe from their federal positions, but Ahidjo refused, probably because he had no desire to embroil himself in the West's factional fights.

10 Ardener, *op. cit.*, pp. 332–333.

Muna and Egbe then formed their own party, the Cameroon United Congress (CUC), to give them a voice in both the Western Assembly and the impending party talks. Finally, to complete the rapid sequence of events, in August the KNDP and CPNC formed a "national government," within which Dr. Endeley was returned to ministerial rank as Leader of the House. N. N. Mbile, his long-time aide and most loyal supporter, became West Cameroon Minister of Works. The CUC now became the opposition.

By the beginning of 1966, instead of two parties preparing for union, there were in fact three parties (the UC, KNDP, CPNC) and a parliamentary clique (Muna and Egbe's CUC). From the point of view of President Adidjo and the eastern politicians, the situation could not have been better to give them maximum leverage over the divided factions in the West. From the KNDP's point of view, maintenance of some sort of quasi-autonomous regional politics, depending as it did on a strong, united KNDP, had been foreclosed for the forseeable future. On September 1, 1966, the four parties finally and formally united to make up what came to be called the Cameroon National Union (CNU; in French, Union Nationale Camerounaise—UNC). Included in the CNU from the East side, it must be added, were the remnants of Mbida's Démocrates and Okala's Parti Socialiste Camerounais. The merger, occuring exactly six years after the federation itself had come into being, converted a polity that had sheltered both a multiparty and a single-party system into a *de facto* national single-party regime.[11] East Cameroon had

[11] The term *de facto* is used deliberately. The merger agreement included two understandings that make the conditional sense neces-

been a single-party state since 1962; it was only a matter of four years until the country as a whole followed suit.

The victory was very much Ahidjo's victory. It marked the triumph of his idea of federalism in which local identities might be permitted to continue, but not in parochial isolation (hence the stated policy of bilingualism in all schools, publications, etc.), and in which a single political movement could effectively control men and events in both states. (Certainly, as was suggested by some cynical observers in 1966, Ahidjo's federal idea was not incompatible with maximum control over the West's less ruly politicians and faltering economy.) The ballet of the political parties in the West was over, in any case. There remained one more series of events in 1967 and 1968 (the West Cameroon elections and Muna's final vindication) to demonstrate the extent to which Ahidjo's thesis had in fact triumphed.

First of all, the western elections were to have been held in December of *1966*. At the beginning of that month, President Ahidjo, in a long speech at Buea, gave some indication that all was not well in the West, despite unification of the parties. He attacked those who constantly talked of "regional rights," reminding them that they had voted in 1961 for reunification and not for federation. The fact of the matter was that the CNU-West was being organized by groups of seven representatives from each of the nine administrative divisions of the West, who were detailed to help form the party in their respective divisions. But these

---

sary: (a) any party that so wished could stay out of the CNU, and (b) new political parties could still be formed, as in the past. This noted, it should be added that in light of the merger, it seems highly unlikely that the above provisions will be invoked soon.

organizers were not themselves members of the executive committees of the divisions and constituencies. It was apparently decided that all the national officers of the old parties and all active politicians be kept out of the new structure. As a consequence, the incumbent western legislators, whose very seats would be at stake in the upcoming elections, had no say in either the organization of the new party or the nominating procedures that were to decide the single electoral lists. The fact that all parliamentarians promptly joined the CNU did little to allay their fears that they might be replaced en masse. In any case, the whole situation became so tense and confused that it was decided to postpone the elections one year so that the CNU, the politicians, and the still-simmering rivalries in the West could be sorted out peacefully.

The West's elections finally took place on December 31, 1967. Nominations were made by the CNU National Political Bureau in Yaoundé, and as a result, twenty-four of the thirty-seven incumbents—somewhat more than had been expected—were nominated. All thirty-seven nominees were then submitted as a single slate to the voters. Jua, attempting to explain the new system, said that the nominating procedure constituted "rather a pre-election and the people are thereafter called upon to signify their approval by voting." [12] There were no surprises in the vote, and soon thereafter the President appointed Muna to replace Jua as prime minister of the West state. Muna, in turn, reduced his cabinet from fourteen to eight, and all but two members of the last government were replaced.[13]

[12] *Cameroon Times* (Victoria), Nov. 25, 1967.

[13] For a biographical portrait of Muna, see "The Man in the Schloss," *West Africa*, July 27, 1968, pp. 857–858.

Here then, was the denouément of the long struggle between the "regionalists" and the "federalists"; with the appointment of Muna, federation with East Cameroon began to have its full effect in the West. The year 1967 had been well spent by the CNU, which had successfully used the new regional branch of the party to destroy what was left of the once-powerful KNDP. Jua, as the last symbolic stronghold of West Cameroonian political autonomy, had to give way to superior strength. The process begun at Garoua in 1961 was finally consummated seven years later: the political union of the two Cameroons was now a fact.[14] And almost forgotten in the press of events was Mr. Foncha, who had once wanted an independent West Cameroon, who had then tried to keep some measure of regional political autonomy, and who had been finally forced to watch the dismemberment of his party and the loss of his colleagues' influence from the powerless heights of the vice-presidency. Foncha's isolation as completed in 1970, when Muna, rather than Foncha, was selected to run as vice-president in the federal presidential elections.

[14] A fact that not everyone seems to have accepted with equanimity, if "Griot" is to be believed: "Though in the long run the advantages [of federation] could well outweigh the disadvantages, right now West Cameroonians tend to feel they are getting a raw deal. The influence of the French-speaking East is now, for the first time, really being felt: not only are Yaoundé's powers considerable, but prices have risen considerably; French and Common Market goods are replacing the familiar British or Nigerian goods; the power of East Cameroon is being felt. Good or bad, if West Cameroonians were today given the choice, they might well choose independence— from Nigeria and from the French-speaking east" (*West Africa*, July 8, 1967, p. 880; "Griot" is the pseudonym of *West Africa*'s itinerant correspondent who specializes in French-speaking African affairs).

EAST CAMEROON POLITICS

The political history of East Cameroon since unification can be most easily understood if seen against the backdrop of the same issue that, during the same period, gave West Cameroon politics its particular thrust: the crystallization of regional power and the move to national party consolidation. In the West, the party of reunification, the KNDP, and its leaders found it impossible to impose their will on either their opponents or minority factions in their midst. Under the impetus of eastern pressures, the West moved, albeit reluctantly, to the national party merger of 1966. In the East, the process was much less complex and considerably more direct: President Ahidjo and his Union Camerounaise party achieved both consolidation of power and party unification by sweeping the opposition aside, by co-opting its leaders, and by simply imposing their will whenever and however it seemed most appropriate. These developments proceeded, as it turned out, in two stages: (1) during 1961–1962, the opposition was put *hors de combat* by various devices, and (2) during 1962–1966, the mechanisms for national organizational unification were developed and finally instituted. The post-1966 period is the period of the Cameroon National Union triumphant, the complete victory of the party machine in Cameroon.

The end of the multiparty system, 1960–1962. Although it was still possible by late 1962 to describe West Cameroon as a multiparty system, with an active (though emasculated) opposition, East Cameroon appeared to have shifted from the relatively flourishing multiparty system that had existed in the territory since 1946 to a single-party system, in which the governmental party had driven virtually all its opponents from the field. The change was startling but not wholly unexpected. The number of one-party states had been on the increase, particularly among French-speaking African countries. This fact, plus the advantages, for both political and economic development, that one-party government appears to confer upon leaders anxious to assert themselves nationally and internationally, was probably not lost upon Ahidjo and his colleagues. At the end of 1962 the only unresolved questions of the new political situation were the future of the dwindling opposition forces and whether West Cameroon would also go the way of its federal partner. The first question could not then be answered. To the second, only an incomplete answer was available: Foncha was in fact talking of a merger of the KNDP with the UC and had begun to put additional pressure on the opposition to do likewise.

In an open letter published on June 16, 1962, four leaders of East Cameroonian opposition parties—Charles Okala, former Foreign Minister and secretary-general of the Parti Socialiste Camerounais (PSC); Theodore Mayi-Matip, president of the parliamentary group of the Union des Populations du Cameroun (UPC); André-Marie Mbida, president of the Démocrates Camerounais (DC); and Dr. Marcel Beybey Eyidi, national secretary of the Parti Travailliste Camerounais (PTC)—rejected the concept of a *parti unifié* (unified party) proposed by President Ahidjo. They made common cause in a loose coalition named the United National Front, and in the Manifesto issued a week later in the name of the Front, they said that such unity could be realized only by sabotaging their own parties for the benefit of the ruling Union Camerounaise and would ultimately culminate in a "facist-type dictatorship." Although rejecting the Ahidjo formula, the four opposition leaders affirmed their willingness to work toward the formation of a "united national front" in which there would be "neither conquerors nor conquered and in which the majority and minority would work together towards concrete solutions to national problems."

A subsequent communiqué issued by the President's office announced that "an impressive stock of weapons" had been found in the homes of Okala and Mbida; within three weeks all four leaders were arrested, tried, and convicted on a charge of "inciting hatred against the Government and public authority, inciting conflict between ethnic and religious communities and disseminating news prejudicial to public authorities." [15]

The arrest and trial of the opposition leaders was the penultimate step in a development that began in 1960 with the fusion of the Mouvement d'Action Nationale Camerounaise (MANC) and the Union Camerounaise. This was followed in April 1961 by the disintegration of the Front Populaire pour l'Unité et la Paix (FPUP), a parliamentary group of Bamiléké that included a number of ex-UPC *maquisards* who had accepted collaboration with the government. In the next three months most of its members joined the UC. The group's nominal leader, Minister of State Pierre Kamdem Ninyim, was the first to leave in April. During the following month six more FPUP deputies joined the UC, and by June the group had been absorbed by the UC. Besides Kamden Ninyim,

[15] Federal Information Service Press Bulletin No. 1895, July 4, 1962. It was claimed that six pistols, twelve chargers, one carbine and 168 cartridges were found in Okala's home. Mbida's home was alleged to contain one carbine, two rifles, and eleven cartridges.

the group had included Victor Kanga, former minister of justice and later federal minister of various portfolios, and Happi Louis Kemayou, then president of the Eastern Legislative Assembly.

The parliamentary group of the Démocrates Camerounais similarly suffered severe attrition of its ranks during 1961 and 1962; by June 1962 the Démocrates, who had begun with eight seats in 1960, were down to six. In August 1961, the Union Camerounaise held a "leadership institute" in Yaoundé where a number of speakers, particularly Assalé, Onana Awana, Kanga, and Samuel Kamé (a young party leader), stressed the goal of creating a party that would unite all Camerounians and indirectly cast serious doubt about the ability of parties other than the Union Camerounaise to accomplish this end.[16]

The direction in which the party and the government were heading was confirmed by President Ahidjo in a press conference on November 11, 1962. Ahidjo pointed out that the imperatives of economic development, and of "alleviating misery," had made it necessary for many African states to adopt one-party systems. This system permitted the effective mobilization of "good will, if not the totality of [human] energies." The formation of such a "great unified national movement" would make possible the forging of national unity, hitherto nonexistent. Such a movement must not, of course, be either monolithic or totalitarian. For Cameroon, the President went on,

I say that it is desirable that there be a great unified party. In any case, I personally hope for a great party, a great unified

[16] "Premier Stage de formation des responsables de l'Union Camerounaise, Aug. 1–6, 1961" (pamphlet issued by the *comité directeur* of the UC, Feb. 1962).

movement that will form itself upon an entente between existing parties; a great unified national party that Cameroonians will enter only after having become convinced; a party within which democracy, freedom of expression, freedom of discussion would exist; a party within which many tendencies could exist, but with the understanding that the minority would follow the lead of the majority. I believe that it is possible to reconcile effectiveness with democracy and freedom of thought. I think, even though it be only in the beginning, that such a system is necessary in Cameroon, in Africa.[17]

Finally, Ahidjo expressed the hope that "Cameroonians, Cameroonian political parties, Cameroonian associations would examine each other's points of view and voluntarily settle on a common minimum program agreeable to all."

The first indication that the government intended to employ more forceful means to create national unity was the dissolution of the UPC congress in Yaoundé on January 22, 1962, at bayonet point. The UPC's parliamentary group had already been reduced by the arrest and trial of Deputy Owono Mimbo Simon in 1961 and by the expulsion of another UPC deputy; the elections to fill these seats resulted in vitories for UC candidates. It has been claimed that the UPC candidates actually won these by-elections (in Dja et Lobo and Kribi) but that the UC candidates were declared elected.

In any case, the record showed that even though the UPC favored collaboration with the government, it rejected the *parti unifié*. The UPC's secretary-general, Emah Otuh, offered to join the *parti unifié* in April, but indications are that he did not speak for Mayi Matip or the

[17] *L'Effort Camerounais* (Yaoundé) Nov. 26, 1961, p. 2; translation is mine.

majority of UPC members. At the PSC congress at Ntui in March, Okala characterized the *parti unifié* as a "play on words," the *parti unique* in a different guise. He indicated that he and the Socialistes were prepared to support Ahidjo but implied that such support depended on a continuation of the "political dialogue."

On April 24 the Federal Assembly met for the first time. The forty eastern and ten western members represented the ruling parties in the East and West Cameroon, constituted into a single parliamentary group, the Group of National Unity. The absence of opposition members from the eastern and western legislatures occasioned some comment, but, according to H. L. Kemayou, president of the Eastern Assembly, the situation provided no cause for alarm since the Federal Assembly was "very representative." Significantly, both Mayi and Mbida had refused to participate in the selection (from the East's legislature) of the forty eastern representatives to sit the Federal Assembly.

By mid-May 1962, Okala, Mbida, Mayi, and Beybey Eyidi (whose Parti Travailliste Camerounais was only forty-five days old at the time) had made common cause in their United National Front, and on June 16 and June 23 they issued the letter and Manifesto that ultimately led to their arrest. It may be added that the four opposition leaders were arrested under the provisions of an anti-subversion law promulgated only two months earlier. The new law provided stringent punishment (imprisonment of one to five years and/or a fine of between 200,000 and 2,000,000 CFA francs) for interference with public authority, for incitement against the federal or state governments, for participation in "subversionary activity," and for starting or passing of false news, rumors, and reports (whether tendentious commentaries or news) injurious to public authorities. Repetition of the offense entails a compulsory jail sentence, and if the offender is a member of the military services or a public official, he is debarred from ever serving in the military or holding any public office again.[18]

Regardless of the truth or falsity of the government's charges against the opposition, and however one interprets the refusal of the opposition parties to join in the *parti unifié,* there is no question that by July 1962 East Cameroon had become, for all intents and purposes, a one-party state. Nothwithstanding the continued presence of opposition deputies in the Eastern Assembly, the opposition in East Cameroon had been so restricted that, at least insofar as its ability to challenge the government and the UC was concerned, its voice on the eastern political stage had become quite feeble. This does not mean that opposition to the regime or to the UC ceased to exist by mid-1962, but simply that organized opposition in the formal political arena had been virtually nullified by that time. What was

[18] At their trial, Mbida, Mayi, Beybey, and Okala attempted to invoke their parliamentary immunity. The court refused to accept the plea, whereupon the four abandoned their defense. They were each fined $980 and sentenced to two and a half years in prison. The government, speaking through J. Bikanda, Commissioner-General for Information, maintained that the four had been plotting against the government and that "they did not hesitate to contact foreign embassies whose help they sought to support their criminal action" (*Afrique Nouvelle,* [Dakar] July 20–26, 1962, p. 6). Six months later, the four appealed their case and had their sentences extended six months and their fines doubled (*Bulletin Quotidien de Presse,* No. 281 [Dec. 6, 1962]).

perfectly clear, in any case, was that the government was serving notice to the remaining opposition groups that their days were numbered.

Consolidation, 1962–1966. The opposition was not un-impressed. During the six months following the imprison-ment of the four leaders, five UPC deputies, two Social-istes, and three Démocrates joined the Union Camer-ounaise. Other well-know opposition leaders not then in the legislatures also switched allegiance: Mathieu Nguélé (former president of the Démocrates), Jacques Ngom (old UPC supporter and former secretary of the CGTC), Emah Otuh (former secretary-general of the UPC), as well as entire organizations such as the Ngondo (tribal organiza-tion of the Douala) and the Union Tribale de N'tem et Kribi. However these and other members of the opposition were persuaded to join the UC (there are indications that positive material inducement, threats, and some exemplary violence were used) by the beginning of 1963 the ranks of the opposition in the Eastern Assembly had been reduced to seven deputies: six Démocrates and one UPC member.

Of the opposition groups, none experienced greater difficulties than the Démocrates. Since Mbida was forced from the premiership in 1958, they not only lost votes to the UC, but with Mbida in jail, they were again leaderless, as they had been when he fled the country in 1959, briefly joined the UPC exiles in Conakry, then returned in 1960 after a reconciliation with Ahidjo. Their new troubles in-cluded the defection of their deputies, and more serious, what appeared to them a deliberate campaign of harass-ment to prevent them from electing their people to local, regional, and national offices. They claimed, for example, that in the by-election of December 1961 their candidate for the Djoungolo (Yaoundé) Assembly seat actually won a majority of the votes, but that the results were altered to favour the UC candidate, Gallus Fouda. They also claimed chicanery in the voting in local elections in Yaoundé and Douala a year later: times were changed, voting booths were moved without warning, etc. In 1964 the Démocrates seriously considered withdrawing their list of candidates for the federal legislative elections of 1964 on the basis of a vague promise for a guaranteed number of seats of the forty to be elected in the East. Besides, the electoral law appears to have been devised to discourage opposition to the UC. The Démocrates finally contested seats in only one of the five constituencies, the south-central, which included Yaoundé, and lost by a margin of two to one: the UC received 388,594 votes (64.8 per cent) of a total 522,136 cast.[19] The loss constituted the Démocrates' last gasp as a party; by the 1965 state elections they had become reconciled to the inevitable. Harrassed by the government, prevented from filing candidatures in time, they endorsed the single lists presented to the voters. The UPC, by then, had also seen that its cause was hopeless, and it also endorsed the single lists. All that remained was the formal union of East and West parties, an event to take place in 1966.

The single party: 1966 and after. On June 11, 1966, Ahidjo convened in Yaoundé the leaders of the three West Cameroon parties, as well as the two regional prime ministers, to urge an end to procrastination on the final merger of the parties. The leaders agreed to the dissolution of

[19] *West Africa*, No. 2660 (May 16, 1964), p. 543. I am grateful to Willard Johnson for much of the material on the Démocrates discussed in this paragraph. See his *Cameroon Federation*, pp. 254–256, for further details.

their several parties and to the final creation of a new national party, the Cameroon National Union. A Steering Committee of thirty was set up to oversee the transition, while a Working Committee of twelve prepared the new party's statutes. The West's representation on the latter committee indicated the new political realities in the state: included were Emmanuel Egbe Tabi, of the CUC, who chaired the Drafting Committee; Samuel Endeley, Dr. E. M. L. Endeley's brother and a lawyer representing the CPNC; Dr. Bernard Fonlon and Nzo Ekah Nghaky represented the KNDP. The other seven were from the East and the Union Camerounaise. On July 23 the draft party statute was approved by the Steering Committee, which then proceeded to set up a provisional executive committee to lead the new party. Ahidjo became president; Foncha and East Prime Minister Tchoungui became vice-presidents; Samuel Kamé, one of the leading party spokesmen, became secretary-general, and Moussa Yaya, a long-time colleague of Ahidjo and party faithful, Ekhah Nghaky, and Egbe Tabi were named assistant secretaries-general. Endeley was not included. In the meantime, the KNDP, CPNC, and the CUC held their last conventions and dissolved themselves. On September 1, 1966, the Cameroon National Union (CNU) came into being, and not long thereafter both the Démocrates and the Socialistes were officially dissolved and then merged with the new party. As for the UPC, its final act of submission came in September 1968, when Theodore Mayi Matip, out of jail since 1965 and presumably reconciled, joined the CNU. Okala, Beybey, and Mbida, the other opposition leaders jailed in 1962, were also released in 1965. Okala quickly made his peace and assisted at the dissolution of his Socialistes. His reward was an ambassadorship. Dr. Beybey Eyidi returned to his clinic in Douala, where he died in 1966. That left Mbida as the sole opposition leader of any note in Cameroon—exiled UPC leaders continued to seek support abroad—who remained outside the embrace of the new party.[20]

At this point, with the single-party system triumphant, it may be useful to look back briefly at the eastern parties that finally, and in some cases with discomfort, merged to become the Cameroon National Union. Such an exercise is useful for more than academic reasons: the parties brought relatively well-defined constituencies and interests to the union, and an understanding of the CNU requires awareness that its constituent groups are not necessarily natural partners. Indeed, the future of the CNU may well

---

[20] The Havana-based secretariat of the tricontinental Afro-Asian-Latin American Peoples' Solidarity Organization (AALAPSO) reported the "first military meeting of the Cameroons guerillas," at which Woungly Massaga (one of the exiled leaders) claimed he was organizing the UPC's "second front" in southeastern Cameroon, and that the "first front," in the Bamiléké area, was led by Ernest Ouandié (*West Africa,* May 25, 1968, p. 620). What was left of UPC guerilla activity by 1969 was in fact highly sporadic and of little threat to the security of the country. (As it turned out, Ouandié was in fact in Cameroon, but not Woungly Massaga.)

Following his release from prison, Mbida apparently suffered a nervous breakdown and went to France for treatment and rest. In April 1967, he returned home, and at a gigantic welcome-home party attended (according to reports) by 5,000 people, publicly declared that thenceforth he would behave so "that no one might say that he was opposed to President Ahidjo." The President, he said, had his support for the great work he was trying to accomplish (*Afrique Nouvelle,* [Dakar] April 7–14, 1967, p. 4). Mbida did not, however, support Ahidjo *unconditionally,* or join the CNU.

depend on the extent to which the formal party union produces cooperation—if not integration—among those groups, constituencies, and interests.

The Union Camerounaise. The founding of the Union Camerounaise as a political party took place in May 1958 at Garoua, where Ahidjo, formerly Vice-Premier and Minister of the Interior under Mbida, and newly installed as Premier (February 1958), convoked a meeting of five small local northern political groups. The parliamentary base of the new party consisted of the twenty-nine northern deputies who already made up the Groupe d'Union Camerounaise plus five others *apparentés* (electorally allied) to the UC group. The twenty-nine UC deputies were mainly Muslim Fulani from the six northern regions (Adamawa, Benue, Bamoun, Diamare, Logone et Chari, and Margui-Wandala) and represented roughly 250,000 voters, about one-third of the total who cast their ballots in December 1956. The 1960 general elections gave the Union Camerounaise fifty seats in eight departments, with the northern administrative units (now increased to seven) yielding about 600,000 votes or roughly 43 per cent of those cast. (The UC actually gained 45 per cent of the total vote.) The fifty seats, it may be added, gave the UC half of those in the National Assembly. In short, even though the UC's seats had increased to seventy-seven in April 1962 because of defections from the other parliamentary groups, its base of power remained the northern constituencies.

Several factors in the northern Cameroonian political situation help to explain the UC's hold in the northern departments. The northern electorate is mainly composed of Musim Fulani; ethnic solidarity must be counted as a positive force tending to electoral conformity. The "Kirdi," who constitute the numerical majority in the north, are still largely unpoliticized, but the UC sought out the more modern element among them. Moreover, the northern traditional chiefs—*lamibé* (plural of *lamido*), emirs, sultans, and so on—aligned themselves with Ahidjo, persuaded that continuing UC rule provided them with the best chances of survival in the face of the inevitable modernization of their areas. Their influence upon their traditional followers is still considerable, a fact attested to by the presence of several northern traditional chiefs in the Eastern and Federal assemblies. Finally, the UC, as the first political party in the north, was the principal avenue to the national political arena and its tangible rewards. The party has been, and in its new guise continues to be, one of the most important modernizing forces in the north and one of the few channels available to young northerners seeking education, advancement, and a chance to participate in the development of the country.

Building upon its northern electoral base and on its control of the government, the UC became a mass party incorporating not only its northern followers but the leadership and, presumably, the following of a number of erstwhile parties. Thus assimilated have been the Paysans Indépendants, the Action Paysanne, the Mouvement d'Action Nationale Camerounaise, the FPUP, and several so-called traditional ethnic-based organizations such as the Union Bamoun, the Kolo-Beti, and Charles Assalé's Association Bantoue Efoula-Meyong. At the fourth party congress at Ebolowa in July 1962, the treasurer-general claimed 300,000 dues-paying, card-carrying members. Even if some exaggeration is granted, the figure still represents the largest number of adherents ever claimed for a political organization in Cameroon. Not even the UPC in its prein-dependence heyday claimed more than 100,000 members.

Until 1966 the party was organized according to a simple hierarchical pattern. The base was composed of a large number of cells grouped under base committees, operating at the village or *quartier* (a neighborhood whose residents are usually of the same ethnic background) level. The latter operated under the direction of subsections responsible to the sections, one of which heads the party organization in each of East Cameroon's departments. Once each year the sections sent representatives to the party congress, the highest formal organ of the party. The congress elected the party's *comité directeur* (executive committee) and the *bureaux* (administrative boards) of the sections and subsections and was supposed to define the party's program and general policies. In practice, the *comité directeur* was the party's principal elaborator of program and principle; in recognition of this fact that the party's locus of power was in the *comité directeur,* the congress was content to be a ratifying, rather than an initiating, body.

Until 1962, the Union Camerounaise could not be said to have had an official ideology; the simple goals of independence, reunification, and reconciliation, plus a more general evocation of the conventional African nationalist demons (colonialism, neocolonialism, imperialism, and so on), sufficed as the party's ideological and programmatic platforms. With the attainment of both independence and (partial) reunification and with the legal reappearance of the UPC on the national scene, the old goals had been attained. As the party in power, the Union Camerounaise began after October 1, 1961, to seek an official ideology suitable to its status and to a less revolutionary atmosphere.

During his four-hour report to the fourth party congress in July 1962, Ahidjo sought to define such an ideology by inventing a millennial Cameroonian and then suggesting the means of his creation:

The sensitive man, the emotional man, the spiritual, religious man; in other words man arising of men, man in society, man strong and proud, even arrogant [only] because of the noble thoughts and ideas he holds—in sum, the man of imperishable spirit constitutes the supreme aim of our entire enterprise. Thus have I tried to define our conception of life.

To explain our ideology in twentieth-century terms, let us say that the theme of all our reflections, of all our political philosophy, both economic and social, is a socializing humanism or, in other terms, African socialism.

For us, Africans—as my friend Senghor has said—nothing that is material constitutes an end in itself. So it is that money, goods, technology in all its aspects have no value for us, Negro-Africans, except in the measure that they have a meaning in human and social utility.[21]

Ahidjo's report is interesting not only for what it contains but also in that it marks the appearance of the Cameroonian President in a new role, that of chief party ideologist. Now a self-confident, vigorous individual, Ahidjo climbed the long ladder to political success without having had the benefits either of higher education (he completed secondary school in Yaoundé) or of a profession

[21] *L'Effort camerounais,* July 15, 1962, p. 3; translation is mine. The report was subsequently reprinted by Présence Africaine, in Paris, as a book: *Contribution à la construction nationale* (1964). The CNU, in 1968, published the *Political Philosophy of Ahmadou Ahidjo,* which elaborates the same themes.

likely to lead him to politics (during World War II he was employed as a radio operator by the government). During his rise to power, he used his considerable political talents to fashion a highly effective political machine from the young, antitraditional elements of the Cameroon north. Articulate, highly intelligent, Ahidjo still occasionally displays an ingrained shyness and aversion to personal ostentation.

The various party congresses, in addition to hearing Ahidjo's annual disquisition, elected the party *comité directeur*. The personalities for the top positions have always reflected with accuracy the relative importance of the UC's leaders both in the party and in the government.

Ahidjo and Arouna Njoya (most recently, Federal Minister of Justice) were, so to speak, the party's founding fathers. In the party, as in the government, Ahidjo exercised full control; Njoya, as a founder of the party, was Ahidjo's second in command and, until recently, probably exercised the next most influential voice in party affairs. Moussa Yaya, Mohaman Lamine, Sanda Oumarou, and Sadou Daoudou were all members of a small inner circle of the party faithful: they are all Ahidjo's men, they owed their positions to him and were schooled under his auspices in politics and in the uses of power. Of the group, probably the most important until recently was Moussa Yaya, whose rise in the party suggested to some observers that he was being groomed for one of the top government positions. Charles Assalé, former Prime Minister of East Cameroon, owed his position to the old MANC's presence in the governing coalition of 1960 and to the fact that he represents important cocoa growers' associations in the Ebolowa area and also the powerful Association Bantoue

Efoula-Meyong, which speaks for most Bulu, Beti, and Eton south of Yaoundé. Assalé was instrumental in persuading MANC to merge into the UC. His position in the party, however, appeared to be largely honorific, since he has never been considered to be close to Ahidjo and the inner circle of northern Muslim Fulani party leaders.

Two southerners, Charles Onana Awana and Victor Kanga were also Ahidjo's men, but in a special sense. Both are technicians—Onana Awana a talented administrator and financial expert, Kanga an attorney and a civil servant —with relatively little political skill. Onana Awana never ran for office, and Kanga won his seat by the most narrow of margins. Dynamic and aggressive, the two men represented the young professional bureaucracy that Ahidjo brought into the government and the party after independence. They may, in fact, have been too aggressive to suit the Cameroonian "old guard," and their fall from grace— Kanga to prison (see p. 157) and Onana Awana in "exile" as Cameroon's representative to the UDEAC—was interpreted in some Yaoundé circles as a warning to the prematurely ambitious. A "rehabilitated" Onana Awana came back to the federal government in June 1970 as Minister of Planning and Territorial Improvement. Henri Effa, Silas Mbong-Bayem, Julienne Keutcha, Richard Manga Mado, and Wanji Nkuimy were members of the growing group of UC "notables" recruited from the opposition parties and associations. Their influence within the party was considered to be minimal, for the very good reason that although they were needed to demonstrate the UC's national character, there was some suspicion that they were in the party as a temporary convenience and were not wholly dedicated to it or its leadership.

The opposition. As of 1966, there has been no formal opposition either to the federal and state governments, or to the single party, the Cameroon National Union. The manner by which the various western and eastern groups were reduced and finally absorbed by the dominant Union Camerounaise to become the CNU has been discussed in some detail. But the old eastern opposition, at least from 1960 to 1966, deserves some notice because of its role in crystallizing the internal politics of East Cameroon (and in the case of the UPC, to a lesser extent, that of West Cameroon as well) and because, as was suggested earlier, its leaders have become part of the ruling amalgam. That opposition, it should be pointed out, has always been rather difficult to define. It included not only the formal parties, such as the Démocrates and the UPC, but various associations with implicit or explicit ties to the opposition parties, as well as the so-called *maquis* groups sporadically active in the southeast and southwest, plus what is left of the old exiled UPC *"durs"* who profess to speak for the "true" UPC, and who insist that they are still directing guerilla activities in East Cameroon.

Cameroon, as UPC First Secretary Emah Otuh pointed out in his speech before the ill-fated January 1962 party congress, was the only example in Africa where "the party which won the struggle for independence" was not represented in the government. Insofar, at least, as it was the UPC that first championed Cameroonian nationalism, and insofar as its techniques, slogans, and program later constituted the basis of action of other parties, Emah Otuh's contention has some justification in the facts. Whatever the case for a "neglected UPC," there is little question, however, that the revived UPC lacked its former militancy, that its leadership was split, that its membership fell off, that its program floundered in vague negativisms, and that its mass appeal dwindled. Some of these difficulties, were exemplified in the split between the party's parliamentary leadership, which included Theodore Mayi-Matip, the "legal UPC's" titular chief, and the younger, more militant wing of which J. P. Sende was representative. The Mayi wing sought to play the role of the responsible opposition; the younger wing demanded more vigorous opposition and a return to the old revolutionary *élan* which characterized the party in preindepedence days. The January congress, it should be noted, was convoked by a provisional national directorate and sought to heal the intraparty breaches which had developed since independence. There are indications that the forcible dissolution of the congress and Mayi's subsequent arrest did little to heal these divisions.

On one subject, at least, all members of the legal UPC appeared to be in agreement, that is, in their condemnation of continued terrorism and of the Conakry exiles who described Mayi and his colleagues as "imperialist stooges." Emah Otuh, in January, stated that the "outside UPC" was itself riven by dissension and that its members were "poorly informed of national realities." He also accused them of "deceiving international opinion and spreading the information that certain regions in the Cameroun were in the hands of the pseudo Army of National Liberation." [22]

Johnson notes that in 1960 the external UPC leaders in Conakry met specifically to discuss the poor coordina-

[22] *Afrique Nouvelle* (Dakar), Jan. 24, 1962, p. 6.

tion and conflicts among the *maquis* groups in Cameroon.[23]
The story of the UPC revolt and the fate of its leaders
has been told elsewhere; [24] suffice it for our purposes to
note that the exile UPC continues to exist, but as a hand-
to-mouth affair, and only because various external friends
—Cuban, Chinese, Guinean, Algerian, Egyptian, etc.—
continue to subsidize it to some extent. The founder of
the UPC, Um Nyobé, was killed in 1958; his successor,
Dr. Félix Moumié was poisoned in Geneva in 1960; and
Moumié's successor, Abel Kingué, died in Cairo in 1965.
The "legal" UPC leaders have all gone over the UC-CNU;
still others were discredited, arrested for conspiracy (Deputy
Owono Mimbo Simon), or removed for nonpolitical crimes
(as was the case with Pierre Kamdem Ninyim, who was
shot for being an accomplice to a murder). What remains
are such old timers as Woungly Massaga, (who flits be-

[23] Willard Johnson, "The UPC in Rebellion: The Integrative
Backlash of Insurgency" (unpub. paper, 1967). See also his "The
Union des Populations du Cameroun in Rebellion," in Robert Rot-
berg and Ali Mazrui, eds., *Protest and Power in Black Africa, 1886–
1966* (New York: Oxford University Press, 1970).

[24] See my *Cameroons from Mandate to Independence* (Berkeley
and Los Angeles: University of California Press, 1964), pp. 141–200,
passim; Johnson, "The UPC in Rebellion"; and my study of the
Cameroonian insurgency, "Cameroon (1955–1962)" in Doris M.
Condit and Bert H. Cooper, eds., *Challenge and Response in Internal
Conflict* (Washington, D.C.: American University, Center for Research in Social Systems, 1968), III, 239–267. A French account is by
Colonel J. Lamberton, *La Pacification de la Sanaga-Maritime:
Décembre 1957–Janvier 1959* (Paris: Centre des Hautes Etudes
d'Afrique Moderne, Etude 3760, 1961). A highly pro-government
account of the UPC opposition and its activities may be found in
Béat Christophe Baeschlin-Raspail's *Ahmadou Ahidjo, pionnier de
l'Afrique moderne* (Yaoundé: 1968), pp. 11–59.

tween Havana, Algiers, and Cairo), Martin Tchapchet (who teaches French in Accra) and Ernest Ouandié (in the Cameroon *maquis* until his capture in August 1970), plus a handful of younger revolutionaries who, because they cannot or are afraid to return, remain in exile continuing "the national liberation struggle." Even these few remnants spend much of their time in ideological squabbles.[25]

In April 1960, the UPC polled about 150,000 votes in the eleven departments where it ran candidates and won eight seats in the National Assembly. Most of its strength was concentrated in the departments of the southwest, particularly in Douala and other southern towns. In December 1960, it claimed 30,000 members, undoubtedly a highly exaggerated figure. The party had substantial support in the departments of Kribi, Dja et Lobo, Sanaga-Maritime, and Nyong et Kellé and was able to muster 800 delegates to the January 1962 congress.

The Démocrates, it will be recalled, reconstituted the elements of Louis Aujoulat's old Bloc Démocratique Camerounais and in 1957 formed the basis of André-Marie Mbida's short-lived control of the government. In its heyday, the party had been able to draw strong electoral support from the heavily Catholic Yaoundé area and enjoyed the support of the Catholic hierarchy throughout the country. Since Mbida's fall from power, the PDC has seen progressively leaner days. During Mbida's voluntary exile to Conakry, from which he returned early in 1960, the

[25] See Abel Kingué's angry response to an article written by some pro-Moscow *Upécistes* (UPC militants), attacking the pro-Peking (Kingué) wing of the exiles: "Réponse à la Nouvelle Revue Internationale," *Révolution* (Paris), No. 12 (Oct.–Nov. 1964), pp. 24–26.

party fell apart organizationally and was held together only by its parliamentary members.[26] His return reinfused some vitality into the party—he was even offered a ministry, which he declined—but his efforts did little to prevent the party from disintegrating still further. Members of the PDC parliamentary group were included in Ahidjo's first 1960 government, though they were soon expelled when their overt criticism became embarrassing to the government.

In 1961 and 1962 several of the PDC's parliamentary deputies defected to the UC, and Mbida developed a very strong antipathy toward the government and Ahidjo. In January 1962 the newly enthroned Archbishop of Ya-oundé, Jean Zoa, was reported to have purged the Yaoundé hierarchy of pro-Mbida followers and thereby completed the Cameroon Church's dissociation from the Démocrates. (The Church did not, however, disengage from political life. In 1963, Zoa was alleged to have had meetings with various political leaders, and in August 1970, the Bishop of Nkongsamba, Msgr. Ndongmo, was arrested and tried for aiding Ouandié and his *maquis*. The Ndongmo affair is discussed below, p. 130.) The party garnered 63 per cent of the votes from Nyong et Sanaga (Yaoundé and its environs) in the April 1960 elections and in December of that year claimed 30,000 active members.

[26] Mbida was implicated in a murder committed by some of his followers and left the Cameroun of his own will. In Conakry he consorted with the leaders of the exiled UPC—Moumié, Ouandié, Kingué—and even signed a declaration of common purposes with them. Unable to come to terms with them, however, and lured by the government's reconciliationist attitudes, he returned home in January 1960.

The Parti Socialiste Camerounais never enjoyed much popular support in Cameroon. Okala, the party's leader and one-time vice-president of the Mouvement Socialiste Africain, was its principal representative in the various Cameroonian assemblies and governments. Despite a claim of 2,000 members and 4,000 *sympathisants* in 1960, the party was largely the organizational handmaiden of Okala. It provided him with a platform for his pronouncements, a staff of campaign workers, and the appearance of a mass following to echo his positions. There is, of course, nothing new in this sort of party in Cameroon; many prominent Cameroon politicians have utilized the pseudo party, the personal organization, for their own political ends. André Fouda, the mayor of Yaoundé, Paul Soppo Priso, once president of the Cameroun's Territorial Assembly (in 1953), Charles Assalé, Martin Abéga, Mathias Djoumessi, and Daniel Kemajou, among others, have availed themselves of this device to further their political careers. The most recent example—the fourth member of the United National Front—is the Parti Travailliste Camerounais, formed in March 1962 by Mbandja Malanga and Dr. Beybey Eyidi. Mbandja is a former UPC activist. Beybey was a Douala physician with a long history as a political lone wolf supporting the UPC. He enjoyed considerable popularity among the immigrants in Douala, particularly in New Bell, where his clinic was located.

Beyond the old political parties of the opposition, the shape of most of the various groups and interests that could be said to be in opposition becomes increasingly blurred. Part of the difficulty lies in their low visibility, a function of their present unwillingness to be seen or heard in a situation in which being in opposition is not without its dangers. Under the circumstances, then, it is possible only to suggest the general social and economic areas in which they can be found; and even this is to do no more than make an educated guess of present attitudes in light of past positions. With these reservations, a few likely pockets of opposition can be discerned: (1) some labor unions, particularly those with former UPC ties; (2) ethnically linked commercial interests in the southwest, especially in the Douala, Kribi, Ebolowa, and Nkong-samba areas; (3) several traditional groups in the south and southwest who see the Ahidjo regime as a threat to their power; (4) a large percentage of Cameroon students studying abroad, since some of the most articulate pro-UPC, antigovernment criticism has come from Cameroon students in France, England, Nigeria, and elsewhere; (5) many discontented, highly politicized urban dwellers, found particularly among the unemployed and the immigrant Bulu, Ewondo, and Bamiléké groups; and (6) other discontented groups, in both rural and urban contexts, that are as yet unreconciled to the present regime or its leaders. In general, then, and despite the ostensible electoral and organizational strength of the CNU, there probably remains some opposition to the regime, concentrated mainly in the southern departments. This opposition, as was suggested, has now largely submerged; how much longer it will remain so and whether the government can eventually win it over are questions which cannot now be answered.

More easily described than the "submerged" opposition is the visible extraparty opposition: the dwindling number of UPC exiles, who have steadfastly refused all offers of amnesty and reconciliation, and the bands of *maquisards* and terrorists still operating at large. The titular leader of the "external" UPC was Ernest Ouandié, once the UPC's national vice-president and in exile since 1955. Ouandié appears to have slipped into Cameroon from time to time to direct operations of *maquis* bands, and according to the government, remained in the country after 1961. In August 1970 he was captured at Mbanga by government security forces; four months later, a military court sentenced him to death for his guerilla activities. He and two other of his colleagues in the *maquis* were executed on January 15, 1971. Except for Woungly Massaga and Nicanor Njague, living in various capitals such as Havana, Ouandié represented the last "name" leader of the illegal UPC wing at large.

Despite the repeated avowals of the Cameroon government that terrorism has definitely declined and indeed altogether disappeared in some sections of the country, reports continue to come from Cameroon that guerilla activity is still somewhat of a problem. At one time guerilla activity was intense in the Bassa ethnic areas of the Sanaga-Maritime, in the southwest, and in the main towns of the south center and southwest. When, in 1958, the founder of the UPC, Ruben Um Nyobé, was killed, the Bassa phase of the revolt ended. Thereafter, except for occasional outbursts of violence and terrorism in the big towns, the guerillas operated mainly in the southwestern areas of the Mungo and the Bamiléké departments. As the rebellion faded, guerilla activity became increasingly concentrated in the Bamiléké ethnic areas, and when the guerilla bands were even further reduced in those areas, groups took to infiltrating from Congo/Brazzaville, where the *maquis* leaders had found sanctuary. Before 1961, guerilla groups were able to use the former British Cameroons as sanctuary, but after federation, the hilly areas on the Bamenda Plateau were denied them as well. The terrorists apparently found (and continue to find, though in smaller numbers) recruits among disgruntled Bamiléké and within the *nouveaux arrivés* of the towns. Two sorts of maquis groups must be distinguished. One type includes those led by highly politicized UPC leaders, some of whom were trained abroad in guerilla tactics. One such group, for example, fought a pitched battle with a unit of the Cameroon Gendarmerie on December 3, 1967, near the Lele River, in the Djoum *arrondissement*. Its leader, the economist Osende Afana, was killed in the action. Government sources revealed that UPC *maquis* had been infiltrating from Congo/Brazzaville since 1965,[27] and President Ahidjo, during a tour of the affected border areas a year later, saw fit to denounce the so-called "second front" of the "pro-Chinese" UPC and to reassure his hearers that the *maquis* efforts continued to be in vain.[28] The second

[27] *Afrique Nouvelle,* Dec. 21–27, 1967, p. 4.

[28] *Ibid.,* Jan. 23–29, 1969, p. 7. Congo/Brazzaville is only the latest of the several countries to provide refuge for the exiled UPC. Guinea continues its support, but on a much reduced scale. Ghana was one of the prime staging and training areas for UPC guerillas, until the regime of President Nkrumah was overthrown in February 1966. Other UPC havens have included Sudan, the U.A.R., Algeria, Cuba, Moscow, and Communist China. Guinea and Ghana, in their time, were the most active suppliers of arms to the guerillas. As late as 1965, *Le Monde* correspondent Philippe Decraene reported seeing the heads of two *maquisards* displayed in the marketplace at Loum, and that this grisly display was not considered unusual by the inhabitants. Decraene reported that Ahidjo assured him that "there are only a few [rebel] bands left in the forests, but the rebellion itself no longer exists. . . . The political character of the rebellion has

type seems to consist of bands taking advantage of con-
fusion and unrest to pillage, kill, and steal; they generally
operate under *ad hoc* leadership and without specific
political motivation. The over-all pattern, however, has
been a diminution of guerilla and *maquis* activity, and
the arrest of Ouandié may well mark one of the last gasps
of the fifteen-year-old UPC rebellion.

Finally, mention must be made of the special position of
the Catholic Church in Cameroon. Since its dissociation
from the PDC the Church has officially declared its
neutrality vis-à-vis Cameroonian political conflict and all
partisan matters. That neutrality was difficult to maintain,
however, in the face of political developments during 1961
and 1962, and during these two years the Church came
into open conflict with the government several times. Two
unrelated events illustrate the nature of the uneasy relationship. Early in February 1962, twenty-five of thirty-six
"political prisoners," including some women and children,
who were being moved from Douala to Yaoundé suffocated
in the railway freight car in which they were riding. The
troop detail guarding them was instructed to bury the
bodies in the forest secretly and without ceremony. One
of the troopers, a Catholic, called for a priest to administer
last rites. Word inevitably reached Archbishop Zoa, who
published a pastoral letter in *L'Effort camerounais* calling
for a requiem mass for the dead prisoners. The govern-

---

abated, and what remains is more and more simple banditry" (*Le
Monde*, March 12, 1965, p. 1; translation is mine). The UPC remnants seem also to have fallen prey to the vice of factionalism. There
are, apparently, a "Maoist" wing (aided from Congo/Brazzaville),
and a "Stalinist" wing (helped by Algeria, Guinea, and eastern European countries). See note 25 above.

ment, embarrassed, seized the issue of *L'Effort* and deported its editor, Father Fertin, a French priest. However, nothwithstanding indications that it might do so, the government did not impede celebration of the mass, which hundreds attended despite the early hour.

The government claimed that the Church, through *L'Effort,* was in fact injecting itself into politics and contended that measures taken against the paper and its editor were fully justified. (In May, another issue of *L'Effort* was seized by governmental decree. This time an editorial entitled "What Are Our Liberties?" appeared to be the cause of the government's ire.) Whatever the justice of the government's complaint against the Church and *L'Effort,* the fact remains that the government looks upon the Church, and Archbishop Zoa, with some suspicion. Since the *Effort* incidents, Ahidjo and Zoa have publicly met and praised each other in an effort to dispel lingering doubts about relations between the two.

The Ndongmo affair, in late 1970, underlined once again the uneasy relationship between the Church and the government. If unofficial reports are to be believed, Ouandié, in confessing his crimes after his capture, implicated Bishop Albert Ndongmo as one of his principal local benefactors. It seems that in 1961, when Msgr. Ndongmo was still a parish priest, he was already in contact with the UPC *maquisards*. Over the years he provided aid and shelter to UPC leaders, acted as liaison between the *maquis* UPC and the exiled UPC groups, and met and helped Ouandié himself several times. In addition, in his public and private declarations, he repeatedly denounced the government. The local Church apparently knew something of his activities, but, as Archbishop Zoa admitted just after Msgr. Ndongmo's arrest on August 27, "the efforts of the local Catholic hierarchy could not prevent" this "sad situation." Msgr. Ndongmo was arrested as he stepped off a plane from Rome, where he had been summoned once Ouandié's charges were known and divested of his clerical functions. He was tried in a military court, along with Ouandié and ninety-nine others, and in December he was condemned to death for conspiring to overthrow the government, complicity in a plot to kill President Ahidjo, and subversive acts. Three of the six condemned to death were executed, but Msgr. Ndongmo and two others had their sentences commuted to life imprisonment on January 14, 1971.

Both the government and the Church tried to play down any latent or actual hostility between them and, incidentally, to dampen any anti-Bamiléké overtones in the affair, since Msgr. Ndongmo is himself a Bamiléké. The Church immediately declared its support for the government and disavowed Msgr. Ndongmo, though Pope Paul VI asked for clemency on his behalf. The government brought its charges through Minister of Justice Félix Sabal Lecco, a practising Roman Catholic, who had spent several years as an administrator in the Bamiléké departments, and indicated that it did not hold the Church responsible for the sins of its errant prelate. The affair, despite the conciliatory attitudes on both sides, has not improved the relations between Church and State, and a suspicious government is more suspicious still.[29]

[29] The Ndongmo affair is reported in "Cameroun: L'Eglise contre l'Etat?" *Jeune Afrique,* No. 508 (Sept. 29, 1970), pp. 32–35. While I was in Yaoundé during the first week of April 1971, I was unofficially informed by Church sources that Ndongmo's return to Cam-

The CNU triumphant: the 1969 party congress. The 1969
CNU party congress was held in Garoua, where the Union
Cameronaise had been founded eleven years earlier.[30] The

---

eroon had come as a surprise to both the government and the
Yaoundé hierarchy. Apparently, according to my informants, the
government had known of Ndongmo's activities for some time, had
informed his superiors of the case against him, and had urged that
the Bishop be sent out of the country before it all became public.
An inquest by the hierarchy—again, according to my sources—revealed that Ndongmo could not refute at least that part of the
dossier that linked him with Ouandié and other members of the
UPC. Ndongmo's departure to Rome was viewed with relief by both
the government and the Yaoundé hierarchy, and it was only when
the Bishop was thought safely out of the country that an arrest
warrant was issued against him. It appeared to my informants, however, that Ndongmo and his friends in Cameroon had prevailed
upon the Vatican to let him return home, arguing that his failure
to return would be construed as an open admission of the Church's
complicity in subversion and terrorism. Thus, Ndongmo returned
to Yaoundé, and the government had no choice but to arrest him
as he stepped off the plane. My informants indicated that
Ndongmo's supporters, as well as Ndongmo himself, were convinced
that the government would never dare attack publicly as popular a
bishop as Msgr. Ndongmo.

The government's version of the affair, including the trials and
judgements of Ndongmo, Ouandié, and their alleged accomplices,
was published in several issues of the CNU party paper, *L'Unité*,
particularly in No. 200 (week of Jan. 15–22, 1971). On the eve of
the trials, the "external" UPC published a dossier on its aims,
theses, and activities: *L'UPC parle* (Paris: François Maspéro: 1970).
Obviously designed to evoke sympathy for the condemned, the latter
volume included letters by Ouandié, an interview with Woungly-
Massaga, and a memorandum tracing the various stages of the party's
struggle.

30 For full text of Ahidjo's report, party statutes, composition
of the National Political Bureau, and other details of the congress,
see the special issue of *L'Unité*, No. 119 (March 1969).

congress took place during six days of intense heat, which, as the party newspaper *L'Unité* delicately put it, was "exceeded only by the warmth in everyone's heart." There was no mistaking the self-confidence of the party leaders; only a well-entrenched and secure party would dare require that its militants listen to speeches for six hot days, including a three-hour-and-forty-four-minute (ninety-seven mimeographed pages) report read by President Ahidjo, who is not the best of orators. As befitted the occasion, the congress was attended by foreign diplomats, members of the international press, and representatives from the ruling parties of Dahomey, Gabon, Guinea, Mauritania, the Central African Republic, Senegal, and Chad. The party, in addition to hearing Ahidjo twice (he delivered a half-hour closing speech as well), preparing various resolutions, and elaborating a new set of party statutes (including statutes for the women's and youth auxiliaries), elected a new Political Bureau to replace the provisional Bureau selected in 1966. There were no surprises in the choices, nor was it unexpected that the Bureau contained the most important governmental figures. Those not included found a place in the National Council or the Congress, which latter, explicitly by party statute, includes ministers and secretaries of state, members of the legislatures, and members of the Economic Council. The new Political Bureau of thirty-five included nine members from West Cameroon and twenty-six from East Cameroon. The national president was Ahidjo; the national vice-presidents included Foncha, Dr. Simon-Pierre Tchoungui (Prime Minister of East Cameroon), Enoch Kwayeb (Minister-Delegate for Territorial Administration), and Willie N. O. Effiom, a western minister and former KNDP official. The rest of the Bureau included such western leaders as Muna, Endeley, Jua, Egbe Tabi, and Bernard Fonlon; and such old-time eastern leaders as Moussa Yaya, Charles Assalé, André Fouda (former Démocrate and mayor of Yaoundé), Sadou Daoudou, and Sanda Oumarou. In all, the Bureau included the federal President and Vice-President, the two prime ministers, and a dozen federal and state ministers.

Elections

Since 1966—that is, since the merger of the various East and West parties into the CNU—elections in Cameroon have not had much relevance to the political life of the country, save as occasions when the regime wishes to mobilize an acclamatory, self-confirming demonstration of popular support. The reasons are obvious: when elections cease being genuine arenas of political conflict, when all the salient political decisions are made elsewhere (within the party or the government, or both), elections no longer generate either attention or interest. This has become the case in most states with one-party regimes, and Cameroon is no exception. As a matter of fact, on October 22, 1968, the Federal Assembly prolonged its own life (it was up for re-election in 1969) another fifteen months to avoid distractions from "productive activities," interruptions from the normal duties of the administration, and additional electoral expense.[31]

The Cameroon operates with what is in fact three electoral systems. First, the federal, under which the federal President and Vice-President, as well as the Federal Assembly, are elected. The President and Vice-President, under the terms of the Constitution (Article 9), are elected

[31] *Africa Research Bulletin,* Oct. 1–31, 1968, p. 1207.

on a single list by universal direct suffrage. For purposes of this election, the country as a whole becomes one electoral district. In the elections of March 1965, President Ahidjo and Vice-President Foncha were the only candidates and garnered 99 per cent of the votes. At the March 1970 presidential elections a single set of candidates was again presented to the electors: Ahidjo for President and S. T. Muna (Prime Minister of West Cameroon) for Vice-President. Both were elected by more than 99 per cent of the votes cast. Elections for the Federal Assembly occur at five-year intervals. The first Federal Assembly was chosen from the sitting regional houses; the first elected Federal Assembly took office in 1964 following a campaign that saw the country's last partisan contest. (The Démocrates ran candidates in the South Central election district.)

The other two systems are those for elections to the state legislatures. In East Cameroon, both the Legislative Assembly and the eastern members of the Federal Assembly are elected from five electoral districts, set up in 1964 to replace the twenty-five departmental districts. In both states, the CNU provides a single list of candidates for all the seats in each district. In the state elections of 1965 (East) and 1967 (West), each list was headed by a local party dignitary with both visibility and standing in the district. For example, in the East, Moussa Yaya (former minister and East Cameroon Assembly vice-president) headed the Northern District list of forty candidates, Charles Assalé (former Prime Minister of East Cameroon) the South Central list of twenty-three, and Happi Louis Kemayou (former president of the East Legislature) headed the Littoral District list of eleven.

Seats in the West Cameroon House of Chiefs are not

elective; they go to the incumbents of the most important chiefdoms of West Cameroon. East Cameroon has no analogous institution, but the most powerful northern Fulani *lamibé* find no difficulty being seated in the eastern Assembly.

Suffrage qualifications in the two states are much alike. There are no restrictions as to sex; voters must be over twenty-one years of age, in full possession of their civil rights, and able to prove citizenship. Voting is secret in both states.

Finally, it should be noted that Cameroon's electoral system, theoretically at least, places no formidable legal or other restrictions on electoral contests: under the terms of the party merger of 1966, new parties may be started, and either old or new parties may freely contest any election. As a matter of fact, however, there have been no contests since the Démocrates' final and ill-fated challenge in 1964, and the CPNC's challenge to the KNDP in the West for the 1964 Federal Assembly. In that election, the CPNC garnered about 24 per cent of the total vote. It is the CNU today that nominates, places on the ballot, and, in the final analysis, fills all the available elective offices.

Administration

Both France and Great Britain left their Cameroonian territories with well-organized and relatively well-functioning bureaucracies. In both Cameroon full-fledged administrative structures were created on both territorial and local levels long before independence became a fact; at the moment of French and British departure both Cameroons had the legal and physical impedimenta for a civil service operating along European lines. Independence, however, brought many unanticipated problems. Most of these derived from the fact that in both Cameroons the operating core of the bureaucracy had been composed of European expatriates and that with their inevitable departure in large numbers the two Cameroon governments had to recruit enough Cameroonians to replace them and, possibly even more crucially, to try to operate the bureaucracies under rules and standards they inherited rather than created themselves.

Before the problems facing Cameroon administration are examined, a glance at the formal organization of the system is in order. Technically, only two levels of organization exist, corresponding to the constitutional division of powers: the federal, operating separately from the state systems but cooperating with the local ministries in areas of parallel or joint jurisdiction, and the two state systems, theoretically expected to maintain liaison through the appropriate federal ministries. In fact and in practice, the whole system is much more complicated and operates much less neatly. To begin with, the capstone of the federal administrative system is not so much the federal ministries, but six federal Administrative Inspectorates whose Inspectors report directly to the President through the Minister Delegate to the Presidency in charge of Federal Territorial Administration and Public Service. The powers of these Inspectors are almost plenary in character: they supervise and coordinate the work of all federal officials and departments within their jurisdiction, they may initiate investigations into the activities of any federal official in their areas, they may call upon the police or the armed forces to carry out their duties, they keep track of all activities and correspondence of federal officials. In short, they guar-

antee—given the extraordinary extent of federal powers—
the centralized nature of the system. Five of the Inspectorates are in East Cameroon; West Cameroon was constituted a single Inspectorate. The latter fact has not always
been accepted with equanimity in West Cameroon; the
federal inspector at Buea (in 1971, an East Cameroonian)
has at times been regarded as a sort of viceroy whose
powers challenge those of the regional prime minister.

Second, every department (nine divisions in West Cameroon, thirty *départements* in East Cameroon) has its
corresponding *préfets* and *sous-préfets* (in the west they
are called Senior district officers and district officers), who
perform the dual roles of state and federal officers. The
préfets and *sous-préfets* are all appointed by the President
and administer the applicable federal law and, in that
guise, are federal officials. However, they also report to
the appropriate state ministries and apply state laws, and,
in that sense, are state officers. This duality of role has
not, apparently, caused much difficulty among the administrators involved, since the range of state powers is narrow.
While the pattern was already long-established in East
Cameroon, it was less familiar in West Cameroon, and
caused some concern over the fact that it created yet another centralizing mechanism at the expense of local prerogatives.

Finally, there are the various state and federal ministries,
designated according to function. The federal ministries
are headed by full-fledged "Ministers," state ministries are
headed by "Secretaries of State." The East-West balance
in the federal cabinet formed in June 1970 was 16:3 (excluding Muna), giving the West 19 per cent of the posts.

Of the two states, West Cameroon has probably experienced the less painful administrative transition, though acute shortages of trained personnel caused some difficulties. Prior to unification, the public service was staffed by British expatriates, members of the Nigerian public service, and local Cameroonians. Official policy foresaw the steady replacement of nonindigenous personnel with qualified Cameroonians. In 1958 the Southern Cameroonian House of Assembly endorsed a goal of "100 per cent Cameroonization of employment," but the goal is still a long way from realization. In March 1960, for example, 26 per cent (301) of the 1,160 officers then serving in the various departments of the Southern Cameroons were non-Cameroonians. The percentage was reduced after unification but at the cost of 250 Nigerians and some 80 British staff who have since returned to their respective homes. Less than British senior officials have remained in West Cameroon, in government or the CDC, and a number of East Cameroonian officials have arrived to take up some of the slack caused by the mass departure of the Nigerians. Sizable personnel gaps in the administrative structure remain, however, and it will probably be some time before sufficient West Cameroonians return from schools abroad or are locally trained to take over both the vacant positions and those created since unification.

In East Cameroon the problems of administrative transition, although similar in nature, have varied considerably in scope and acuteness. First, "Cameroonization" acquired political overtones nearly absent in the West Cameroon. For East Cameroonian politicians and officials, Cameroonization—actually pursued with vigor by Cameroonian governments and the administering authorities during the latter years of the trusteeship—represented yet another method of eliminating the French colonial presence and asserting Cameroonian independence. In the hands of Cameroon nationalists, it became a club with which to beat the French when the latter seemed reluctant to speed up withdrawal or a symbol which could be used to flout waning French authority. Overuse of Cameroonization as a political weapon was probably partially responsible, upon the attainment of independence on January 1, 1960, for the departure of a larger number of French officials than had been anticipated, or indeed desired, by the Cameroon government. In 1960 and 1961, increasing numbers of Cameroonians filled official posts; the last French departmental *préfet* left in 1961, and by the end of 1965 no more than 110 French expatriate advisers and civil servants (excluding the personnel of the sizable French military mission) were listed as connected with the Federal services.[32]

[32] *Annuaire national de la République Fédérale du Cameroun* (Yaoundé: Commissariat General à l'Information, 1965). There is some question about the total number of expatriates working for the Cameroonian governments. One report in *West Africa* (April 30, 1966, p. 479) stated: "There are about 700 people paid for by the French Technical Assistance budget, but there are many thousands of French in East Cameroon either kept on by the African administration or (the great majority) engaged in commerce." The *Annuaire national* listed 110 Frenchmen in the federal services, 34 expatriates in the East Cameroon government, 33 in the West Cameroon government service, 3 French *sous-préfets*, and 7 French mayors in the East, a total of 187 expatriates. During a visit to Cameroon in 1965 I was told by an official in the Civil Service Ministry that there were only "about 250 expatriates" in Cameroon government service, on both federal and state levels. An official from the Cameroon Investment Bank said there were "over 500" expatriates in government service. I was unable to verify either estimate. In April 1971, I was told that there were "less than 150"

Recruitment problems largely absent in West Cameroon developed during 1960, 1961, and 1962. Beginning in 1956 France pursued a plan whereby French officials in each department would be gradually replaced by Cameroonian scholarship students who completed their studies in France. Accordingly, some 95 scholarship graduates were returned to the Cameroun in 1956, 71 in 1957, 42 in 1958, 51 in 1959, 14 in 1960, and 27 in 1961. A significant number of these graduated from the two most important administrative training centers in France, the Institut des Hautes Etudes d'Outre-Mer and the Ecole Nationale d'Administration. Most of the rest were trained at various French universities. An unanticipated set of difficulties arose between 1960 and 1964 when it became obvious that many of the new returnees found their expectations shattered by the realities of bureaucratic life. As the trainees returned from France, the better positions at the top were quickly filled, and many young Cameroonians who had anticipated placement at the higher ministerial or departmental levels found themselves relegated to lesser positions with lower pay, fewer prerogatives, and considerably less prestige. Under the circumstances, an increasing number of young graduates have been accepting official posts with reluctance or, if they are free to do so, have sought avenues to success. In some instances, the Cameroon government has even had to resort to severe measures to bring reluctant graduates home from France; in 1961 it terminated the financial support of a number of students.

------

expatriates in government service. Though my source was an official one, I could not confirm the estimate. One problem is that expatriates serve not only in ministries and departments, but in schools, the university, and other official and quasi-official agencies.

Another factor which had considerable effect upon the recruitment program has been the high level of political activity among Cameroonian students in France. A large percentage of them, at least up to 1964, were hostile to the Ahidjo regime and had aligned themselves with the UPC or with left-wing student groups or causes. In all, recruitment to administration has not been as satisfactory as the government might desire; not only do many positions remain unfilled, but the ranks of the younger bureaucracy are becoming more and more restive. Undoubtedly many young officials feel that their ambitions have been thwarted and that the political leadership of the country has not recognized their talents properly. In addition, the government has recruited a large number of individuals who seem ill prepared for their tasks and more concerned with the status of their positions than the performance of their duties.

It is therefore not surprising that many Cameroonians have been keenly disappointed in the performance of their officials. If President Ahidjo is to be believed, the East Cameroon civil service can be charged with nearly the entire catalogue of bureaucratic shortcomings. In March 1962, he excoriated East Cameroon officialdom in a well-publicized memorandum, parts of which deserve to be quoted at length:

A marked laxity among nearly all civil servants is becoming more and more apparent. . . . In the majority of the administrative offices, even up to the central services and the different ministries, there reigns such carelessness and such anarchy that even the least informed and least aware are alarmed and sorely troubled over the future of our civil service. . . .

. . . among these failings are intemperance, dishonesty,

and lack of courtesy; poorly done work, lateness and absentee-ism, lack of discipline and insubordination, . . . inflated re-munerations, and the simultaneous holding of several jobs. . . . Furthermore, civil servants should refrain from overt criticism of and insults to the Government or its policies.[33]

Even allowing for rhetorical exaggeration, Ahidjo's broad-side is remarkable for it frankness.

The civil servants were still a cause for concern some six years later. According to President Ahidjo in a radio interview, many civil servants were chronically in debt at the end of the year and complained that they had not had a wage increase in ten years. He pointed out that in 1966 they had chosen free housing instead of a 20 per cent in-crease in pay, and described their demands as "wanton." He noted that 10,000 million CFA francs of the 1968 budget of 24,000 million CFA francs (41 per cent) had been devoted to administration.[34] Hugon indicates that the income of what he terms the "black political bourgeoisie," a class that includes civil servants, is from ten to a hundred times greater than that of ordinary laborers. For example, the average monthly income of the top two grades of civil servants, in 1965, was 129,867 CFA ($530) and 101,313 CFA francs ($413), compared to 3,558 CFA francs ($14.80) for an agricultural worker, or 5,539 ($21.80) for a domestic servant. [35] Since independence, the East Cameroon govern-

[33] *Afrique Nouvelle,* April 4, 1962, p. 6; translation is mine.

[34] *West Africa,* Aug. 24, 1968, p. 994. It should be pointed out that a 41 per cent slice for administrative expenses is not excessive for Africa. The annual budgets of some countries, such as Dahomey, Togo, and Senegal, devote up to 65 per cent to civil servants.

[35] Hugon, *Analyse du sous-développement en Afrique noire: L'exemple de l'économie du Cameroun* (Paris: Presses Universi-

ment has been confronted with many embarrassing instances of the very misconduct which Ahidjo condemned, a number of which involved high officials.[36] Yet, in all justice and in view of the monumental problems of recruitment, training, Cameroonization, and indoctrination, most East Cameroonian officials have served honestly and effectively even in the face of some flagrant abuses by many of their colleagues. The West Cameroonian civil service, it may be added, has been relatively free from scandal.

Local Government

Under the terms of the federal constitution, the federal government prescribes the forms and authority of local governmental units. The system adopted is an amalgam of patterns carried over from the trusteeship period, based on British and French administrative models, and forms developed in response to the federal structures created in 1961.

---

taires de France, 1968), p. 231. Hugon cites figures provided by a private research concern. These figures are given added force by the fact they represent data taken *in Yaoundé;* incomes at the lower end of the scale tend to veer sharply downward as one leaves Yaoundé or Douala.

[36] Instances of mismanagement were conspicuous in the Ministries of Education, Finance, and Rural Development, for example. The chief customs officer of Douala was arrested, and the chief customs officer of Yaoundé absconded with over 2,000,000 CFA francs in receipts, among them a customs payment from the present writer. Finance Minister Onana Awana instituted draconian measures to curb some of the worst examples of financial irresponsibility, but his fight was only partially successful.

WEST CAMEROON

West Cameroon is divided into nine administrative divisions (in French, *départements*) operating under the Federal Inspectorate at Buea: Fako (formerly Victoria), Ndian, and Momo, in the south and on the coast; Meme (formerly Kumba) and Manyu (formerly Mamfe) in the forest hinterland; Mezam (Bamenda), Mentchum (Wum), Donga and Mantung (Nkambe), and Bui, in the grasslands plateau.[37] In addition, there are twenty-two subdivisions (French, *arrondissements*) and one district (Bali), which operates under the jurisdiction of the Bamenda subdivision. The divisions are headed by senior district officers, the subdivisions by district officers. These officers are considered the western counterparts of *préfets* and *sous-préfets,* and are, like their equivalents in the East, responsible to the chain of command that includes the Federal Inspector, the Federal Administration Bureau (Direction de l'Administration Fédérale), and the Minister for Territorial Administration and Public Service. Within each division, local administration and budgetary control are provided by a popularly elected divisional council functioning under the guidance and advice of the district officer and resident and visiting representatives of the specialized departments of the government. The divisional councils control the operations of subordinate district councils, also popularly elected, whose size varies from division to division. Where tribal authority

[37] The name changes were brought about by presidential decree in February 1969. Momo (formerly Gwofon), Ndian (formerly Nwa), and Bui (formerly Kumbo), which had been subdivisions, were given full divisional status.

systems remain strong, the district councils are ordinarily based upon the recognized traditional authority in the area concerned, usually a chief acting with or without a council. Where there are no customary authorities with power over a wider area than the village—as is often the case, for example, among the forest people—the representatives of extended families or groups have been formed into councils and given statutory powers as district councils.

To a large extent, then, local governmental units at the district level tend to be founded on existing traditional institutions. Thus, where tribal custom and loyalty are strong, the chiefs are capable of exerting considerable influence at local levels of government, and there is no doubt that some of them, notably the powerful grasslands chiefs (the Fons of Bali, Bafut, and Nsaw, for example), have done so in the past. With the growth of party organization, however, it appears that the influence of the traditional chiefs is somewhat on the wane. During the 1961 plebiscite the Fon of Nsaw openly advocated integration with Nigeria, but KNDP campaigners operating in the traditional Nsaw districts engineered a heavy majority for reunification. Finally, in addition to the area-based administrative structures, several of the larger towns such as Victoria, Buea, Kumba, Mamfe, and Bamenda have full-fledged municipal governments composed of elected municipal councils and officers.

EAST CAMEROON

Local government in the eastern state rests upon a tripartite base composed of (1) the classic French prefectural organization, (2) a complex system of urban and rural communes, and (3) an array of minor and major chiefs.

Each of the thirty departments of East Cameroon is headed by a *préfet,* who makes his headquarters in the departmental capital and supervises the local administration of central governmental services of the eastern state. These include education, telecommunications and posts, finances, public works, agriculture, health, and police. The departments are each subdivided into one or more *arrondissements,* and these, in instances where size or population require it, are sometimes divided into districts. *Arrondissements* and districts are under the authority of *sous-préfets* and district heads respectively, officers subordinate to the departmental *préfets.* There are altogether 106 *arrondissements* and thirty-seven districts in East Cameroon.

The communes, special units of local government, are of two main types, urban and rural. Urban communes are either *communes de plein exercice* (with full powers), *communes urbaines de moyen exercice* (with limited powers), or *communes mixtes urbaines de moyen exercice.* The two types of urban communes are created by governmental decree and represent the two stages of development toward the fullest municipal autonomy possible under the law. The communes with full powers are the older, established urban centers (such as Douala, Yaoundé, Nkongsamba, and so on) whose inhabitants already have considerable political and administrative sophistication. "Full powers" represents, in this context, complete control over municipal finances and services. The communes with restricted powers are those urban centers whose inhabitants are not deemed to have attained the maturity required for the status of communes with full powers. The technical difference between the two types consists in the manner in which the chief municipal executive is selected. In the former, the mayor is elected at large from the commune. In the latter, a mayor-administrator is nominated by the Minister for Territorial Administration. Both types of communes have municipal councils elected from common rolls. The third variety of urban commune, the mixed urban commune with restricted powers, is in every way similar to the commune with restricted powers except that an ethnically mixed population may require special rules to determine the selection and composition of the municipal council. Ngaoundéré and Garoua, for example, have municipal councils in which two-thirds of the councilors are elected at large and the other third are "notables" (chiefs and so on) appointed by the Minister for Territorial Administration upon the recommendation of the prefect in whose department the commune is located.

Communes mixtes rurales are a special form of local government, again created by governmental decree. They are usually coterminal in area with *arrondissements* but may be of any size fixed by law. They may also coexist with urban communes, in cases where the latter are physically located within rural communes. The mixed rural commune is headed by a mayor, who is appointed by the Minister for Territorial Administration, and governed by an elected municipal council of fifteen to forty-four members, depending on the population in the commune.

Traditional chiefs continue to play an important role in local government in East Cameroon, particularly in the seven northern departments where no *communes mixtes rurales* have been created. The northern chiefs (*lamibé*, emirs, sultans), with their traditional councils or assemblies, enjoy considerable authority in local affairs and usually constitute the basis of local government in their areas of jurisdiction. In the southern departments, a variety of local chiefs (paramount chiefs, group chiefs, village chiefs, *chefs de quartiers*) either exercise local administrative authority as agents of the central government or participate in communal governments. All chiefs must be officially recognized by the central government and are financially compensated to the extent they perform governmental functions.

The entire system of local government is under the control of the Ministry for Territorial Administration, locally through the officials of the prefectural organizations, and regionally the Federal (Administrative) Inspectors with headquarters in Buea, Yaoundé, Douala, Garoua, Bafoussam, and Bertoua.

Role of the Judiciary

In neither of the Cameroon states has the judiciary shown any tendency toward involvement in the political scene. Two reasons probably account for this fact. One is that the tradition of judicial noninvolvement is very strong in both states; the other lies in the fact that both East and West Cameroonian judicial systems contain numbers of nonindigenous judges, lawyers, and administrators. The East Cameroon Supreme Court and Courts of Appeal, for example, include several French judges sitting under the terms of the 1960 Franco-Cameroonian Convention which provides for their presence until they can be replaced by Cameroonians. Similarly, in West Cameroon, British and other English-speaking judicial personnel form an important component of both bench and judicial administration. Their very visibility has imposed considerable restraint upon them; they tend to perform the tasks required of them quietly and without publicity. This is not to say that their presence does not occasionally stimulate demands for their removal. In May 1962, the CPNC *Cameroons Champion* attacked the West Cameroon attorney general and assistant attorney general and demanded their dismissal. Both were West Indians.

Under the terms of the constitution, the federal government has control of all judicial organs, a provision reflecting a desire for the eventual and complete synthesis of the separate judicial systems the states brought to unification in 1961. One notable step in that direction was the promulgation, October 1, 1966, of a national criminal code embodying an amalgam of the common law and French legal traditions of the two states.

The structure of the judicial system [38] is capped by the Federal Court of Justice. Each state has its own Supreme Court, and a subordinate system of Courts of Appeal (one in West Cameroon, four in East Cameroon), with this difference: the West Cameroon Supreme Court combines the functions of the High Court and the Court of Appeal. The bottom of the judicial ladder is occupied in the West by the Magistrate and Customary Law Courts, in the East by twenty-one Courts of First Instance (*Cours de Premier Instance*), plus Customary Courts in both states. The regular system has multiple jurisdiction: it can try and hear all cases under the civil, penal, commercial, social, and customary law. The system also contains some special military courts, set up during the early days of the federation or before unification to provide what amounted to summary justice to persons caught and convicted of in-

[38] For details, see Enonchong, *op. cit.,* pp. 205–237.

volvement in the UPC rebellion or of some particularly heinous crime. There is a Permanent Military Court in Yaoundé, and several other military courts that may move about the country and increase in number as the occasions for their use arise. These courts, it may be added, do not receive much publicity, since they exist in a sort of constitutional vacuum; nevertheless, some important cases are heard by them. Those accused in the Tombel massacre of December 1967 (see p. 155) were tried in one of the military tribunals, in June 1968 the Permanent Military Court at Yaoundé tried and sentenced to prison some thirteen persons, including six Presbyterian pastors, for subversion and the "dissemination of false news." The trials of Ernest Ouandié and Msgr. Ndongmo were also conducted in one of the special military courts. Finally, the Special Criminal Court, sitting in Yaoundé with nation-wide jurisdiction, hears cases involving embezzlement and misappropriation of public funds. There are also Labour Courts and so-called lower Conciliation courts.

CHAPTER 4

Contemporary Issues

National Unity

In a statement issued following the constitutional talks held at Foumban in July 1961, Premier Foncha spoke of the "existence of two Cameroon cultures," and expressed the hope that by the "process of evolution" the two cultures would eventually be replaced by an "indigenous one." Apart from the question whether two such cultures actually existed, it is probably fair to say that ten years after unification Foncha's "indigenous" Pan-Cameroonian culture had only barely begun to take shape. The differences between the two states may only have been skin deep —or "colonial deep," as someone suggested in 1965—but these were differences that had become part of the fabric of the societies on both sides of the common border between East and West Cameroon. What was involved in this union of the "several Africas," to use Willard Johnson's phrase, were not only differences in language, culture, and institutions, but perhaps most crucial for the union, differences in political habit and perceptions of authority crystallized during seventy-five years of separate colonial experience. Those latter differences, much more than the first group, account for the still visible—though muted— doubts about the federation seen in such things as the Muna-Jua power struggle, the long delay in coming to the national union of parties, and, in general, in the widely-held suspicion that the East wants not only to dominate

152

the West (which it already does) but to absorb it into a unitary state. With all the good will in the world, after all, it is difficult to overlook the fact that East Cameroon is ten times the size of West Cameroon, or the fact that "roughly two-thirds of the . . . West Cameroon current budget comes as a direct subsidy from the Federal Government." [1] This sense of unease may, of course, be only a short-run thing, and in the long run, federation may, as West Cameroonian "federalists" insist, be the best thing that ever happened to the territory. Certainly, by whatever standards one applies, West Cameroon was not a viable economic entity, nor could it forseeably become one. For all these reasons, then, it becomes relevant to examine some of the main areas in which national unity—in the sense of unity between the two states—will have to be accomplished in order to make the federal union a reality. Such examination, in short, seeks the visible progress made toward the goal of which the federation is the ostensible symbol.

Three areas of immediate relevance are institutions, political activity, and economic life. All have already been treated at length, and it becomes possible now to suggest some of the conclusions which can be drawn from these discussions and indicate some additional problems in each area. Excluded from consideration will be the more intangible areas of popular culture, language, or even education (as it relates to teaching citizens the symbols and objectives of national unity).

[1] "Cameroon Complexities," *West Africa*, April 23, 1966, p. 447.

INSTITUTIONS

Until 1965, when Foncha relinquished the prime ministership of West Cameroon, and when the new Federal
Assembly began passing a variety of laws designed to
speed institutional integration, federal institutions appeared to have something of an *ad hoc* character. The
provisional legislative powers allocated the state legislatures over some thirteen items (Article 6) until they were
transferred to the federal authorities, became moot when,
by 1966, most all had been transferred. Police came under
federal control from the beginning, and by 1965, all aspects
of finance and medical and educational services were
securely under federal jurisdiction, either directly or
indirectly. Even local administration, as was noted, came
under federal control with the nationalization of the prefectural and district officer systems. It is probably fair,
therefore, to suggest that by 1969 there were very few
aspects of the two states' administrative, legal, economic,
and financial life there were not under some form of
federal control or supervision.

POLITICAL ACTIVITY

By 1969, almost all state and national political activity
was securely tucked under the CNU umbrella. An obviously impressed German journalist suggested that political activity had become even more centralized:

The State is Ahidjo and Ahidjo is the State. Some say that
Cameroon is lucky that its President is so young; many affirm,
half in earnest and half in jest, that when Ahidjo sneezes,
his twenty-two ministers all catch cold. About one thing no
one jokes: without him, without this son of a Fulani chief

and former radio technician, Cameroon would not have become Cameroon; without his "dictocracy" his "planned liberalism"—thus is the official usage—the country would have long ago gone the way of the Congo or Nigeria.[2]

This much is true: at least by mid-1971, Ahidjo and his regime had no visible opposition. In 1968 Ahidjo celebrated the tenth year of his rule, no mean feat in an Africa already by then littered with dead, deposed, or ousted presidents, prime ministers, and generals. Yet, if President Ahidjo and his government are relatively secure, it is not because the country is completely calm or because there are no longer any vexing political problems. That security rests on the continued supremacy of the party-government machine and its ability to enforce the peace, with what are often severe and (to some) repressive measures. Moreover, after nine years of federation, some of the problems that had previously helped to fan the flames of rebellion were still present, though different in substance, direction, and importance. Of these problems, none is more widely ramified than the ethnic differences that abound in the country and that occasionally flare into violence.

On December 31, 1967, a mob of Bakossi in Tombel ran riot and slaughtered as many Bamiléké as it could find. Tombel is located a short distance into West Cameroon on the Bamenda-Babadjou-Dschang road. First reports in-

---

[2] Dietrich Strothmann, "Unter dem Diktat der Angst," *Die Zeit*, March 18, 1969; translation is mine. The word "dictocracy" is the best rendering I (and the editors of this book) could make of *Demokratur*, the German rendering of *démocrature*, a French compound play on the words *démocratie* and *dictature* (democracy and dictatorship). The meaning of the pun is unmistakable. I heard the term *démocrature* used in Yaoundé in 1965.

dicated that 68 people had been killed, but at the subsequent trial of the persons accused of participation in the massacre, the larger figure of 236 deaths was officially established. The government immediately rushed troops into the area, and clamped down on movement and communication lest Bamiléké come across the state frontier to aid their ethnic brethren. Within two days tensions had abated and order was restored. One hundred and forty-three Bakossi were eventually brought to trial before a military court: 17 were condemned to die by a firing squad, 37 were sentenced to be detained for life, 38 to be imprisoned for life; 10 were jailed for ten years, and 4 were to be detained for twenty years; 36 were freed, and one man died during the trial.[3]

The reasons for the massacre were complex, but this much seems to have been established: the immediate catalyst for the violence was the robbery and murder of four Bakossi, including a schoolteacher, by a group of bandits shortly before Christmas. It was widely assumed that the bandits were Bamiléké, and that this act represented a deliberate provocation by the Bamiléké against the Bakossi. Tensions were already high in the area because of what many Bakossi styled a Bamiléké "invasion" of their area: Bamiléké had in fact come in numbers to

[3] *West Africa,* May 20, 1967, p. 672. This was the first serious mass violence involving Bamiléké since early 1960, when in retribution for the death of some Bamun, an armed group of Bamun crossed the Noun River and killed over one hundred Bamiléké. Unlike the later massacre, perpetrators of the 1960 killings were never brought to justice. One story I heard from a reliable source was that the raid had been sanctioned by the Sultan of Bamun and that he had subsequently received several severed Bamiléké heads as a token of its success.

settle and buy land in the Tombel-Bamenda area, and had begun to control commerce in the area much as had the Nigerian Ibo in the Kumba area to the south. In any case, it was the old *problème Bamiléké* in a new and more deadly guise.

There were overtones of *le problème Bamiléké* in the Victor Kanga affair. Kanga was a Bamiléké, a UPC partisan during his student days, who had risen fast in the Ahidjo regime once he had made his peace with it. Kanga was highly educated; he had earned a *doctorat en droit* from the University of Paris. Upon his return to Cameroon, he first entered the Customs Service, then, after Cameroun became independent, succeeded Charles Okala as Minister of Justice in the first Cameroun Republic. He rose to become Minister of State for National Economy in 1961, then, from 1963 to 1966, served as Federal Minister of Finance. In August 1966, his star began to wane when the President (some say deliberately) reshuffled his cabinet to move him to a less critical position, Minister of Information and Tourism. Kanga was not, apparently, happy with the change in his fortunes, and early in November an anonymous pamphlet entitled "A Victim of Duty" began to circulate in Yaoundé and Douala. The pamphlet alleged that Kanga had been dismissed from his post as Finance Minister because he had wanted to expose misappropriation and other malpractices by certain ministers in Ahidjo's cabinet. On November 22, he was dismissed from his post as Federal Minister of Information and Tourism, and a week later, arrested on charges of "publishing false news." Various rumors spread through Yaoundé after Kanga's arrest, including one about a possible attempted coup by discontented Bamiléké in the government. There was no such attempt, but security precautions were unusually strict during Kanga's four-hour trial in December.

Kanga had originally been charged with sending money abroad illegally, but his trial focussed on the pamphlet, which, it was alleged, he had written and distributed in league with four other (Bamiléké) functionaries, also on trial. Kanga contended he was being persecuted because he had stumbled across damaging evidence of embezzlement, and that those concerned were determined to be rid of him. The State contended that the pamphlet tended to discredit the government.[4] Some eleven persons were convicted on offenses arising from the affair, including two important functionaries, Pierre Tchanké, former Secretary-General of the Ministry of Finance and Joseph Foalem Fotso, Assistant Director of Broadcasting. Both men are Bamiléké. Kanga was convicted and sentenced to four years' imprisonment. Whatever else the Kanga affair proved, it did permit a glimpse of what may be the top of an oppositional iceberg, mostly submerged because of the high cost of overt confrontation. The government of President Ahidjo is sufficiently broadly based to give the lie to the assertion that it is a "northern" regime, but the old north-south antagonisms apparently die hard.

Other signs that the regime itself was not entirely comfortable, though secure in power, included such things as the prosecution of thirteen persons in 1968 for "dissemination of false news," the continued existence of the special military courts, the censorship of news published in the

[4] See H. N. A. Enonchong, *Cameroon Constitutional Law* (Yaoundé: Centre d'Edition et de Production de Manuels et d'Auxiliares de l'Enseignement, 1967), pp. 138–140, for a brief but critical review of the case.

country, and the nervousness displayed by the regime over the continued existence of what is admittedly only a minor residue of the UPC rebellion.

In all, it may take some time before the sort of consensus develops that will undergird genuine national political unity.

ECONOMIC UNITY

As Alan Warmington and others have pointed out, the political union of the two Cameroon states can be justified on purely economic grounds. The excellent communication facilities of the southern East provide advantageous routes of egress for the products of the West, particularly those of the grassfields area. Ethnic ties between the two states provide the basis of expanded and advantageous commercial intercourse. The problems of labor migration, both seasonal and permanent, have long complicated Cameroons-Cameroun relations; the central services of the federal government have become available to solve these problems and rationalize interstate labor exchanges. To all this must be added the fact that the Germans developed the area that includes West Cameroon and southwest East Cameroon as a unit and planned roads, railways, and towns on that basis.

Complete economic unity, of course, has not been achieved, but economic integration is progressing and, as was noted earlier, the outlines of a national economy have begun to take shape. The most important step in that direction was the alignment of West Cameroon's tariff system with that of East Cameroon in January 1966. This permitted the Federation as a whole to apply the tariffs of the Central African Customs and Economic

Union (UDEAC), of which Cameroon is a member. Integration tariffs also meant wholesale application of East Cameroonian taxes. Together the change-over resulted in some considerable dislocations, felt locally in a rise in the price of consumer goods and state-wide in a devaluation of real wages and a decrease in purchasing power. Though it was, for all practical purposes, impossible to provide compensation for all such losses and dislocations, the federal government, through subsidies, increased the wages of West Cameroon government employees and paid for state-wide foodstuff distribution. More important, some of the mainstays of the West's economy, such as the Cameroons Development Corporation, suffered severe setbacks with federation. The CDC lost £2 million of the £3 million loan from the British Colonial Development Corporation (prohibited from lending outside the Commonwealth, which West Cameroon left on federation), and had to borrow capital from the government of Nigeria, as well as float credit from Barclay's Bank and Cameroon Bank. It took a £3 million loan from the World Bank and a £2 million loan from the Development Fund of the Common Market to set "Camdev" back on its feet.[5]

In the final analysis, however, federation has benefited the economy of West Cameroon: the West has been able to tap the aid resources of the Common Market; it has become able to balance its budgets, with federal help; it is now part of a larger planning unit where formerly it had to rely on what amounted to handouts from unreliable sources; and it now has available the educational, social,

[5] The economic problems of the Cameroon Development Corporation are summarized in "Cameroon, Britain, and Nigeria," *West Africa,* May 21, 1966, p. 563.

and administrative services of its better developed and economically stronger partner.

Economic Development

A fundamental preoccupation of Cameroon's leadership, as indeed of most Cameroonians of modern persuasion, is the problem of the economic development of the country. To a large extent, the manifold problems of unification take on new meaning when seen within the context of the larger imperatives of national economic growth. The prevailing official mood, on the whole, was one of optimism that the federation could attain self-sustained growth; the plan elaborated in 1960 foresaw a doubling of the average per capita income in twenty years, the product of a national growth rate approximating 4.6 per cent per annum. The plan was based upon the fulfillment of certain key requirements, such as the full mobilization of human resources and major legislative and administrative innovations, and, of course, the attainment of a number of economic objectives: creation of a north-south communications axis, greater production and consumption of meat animals, refinement of distribution patterns and facilities, increase in the production of primary export products, a higher volume of savings, development of better credit facilities, and full development of the potential for the creation and operation of various types of cooperatives. On their face, the data for Cameroon's economic performance seemed to more than justify the government's optimism. At the 1969 CNU congress, President Ahidjo reported:

If the sum of the Federation's economic activities are taken together, and if the Gross Domestic Product [*Produit interieur brut*—P.I.B.] of 1959 is compared to that of 1965–66, you will note that it moved from 113,000 million CFA [ca. $462 million] to 177,000 million CFA [ca. $722 million], that is, a 56 per cent total increase and an average annual increase of 8.6 per cent, all of which places Cameroon among the countries with the highest development rates.[6]

GDP data do, of course, often conceal more than they reveal, and Cameroon's are no exception,[7] but even Philippe Hugon, who has exhaustively revealed the flaws in the Cameroonian economy, concedes that the overall picture of the economy is a promising one: "Today, under the authority of the Chief of State, of the UC [sic] and the moral forces of the nation, the structures most likely to promote development are in the process of being built." [8]

The key to Cameroon's current efforts to achieve sustained economic growth has been its two short-term de-

[6] *L'Unité* (Yaoundé), special issue, March 1969, p. 4.

[7] For example, the spectacular GDP growth figures do not show that the great increase has been in the monetary sector of the economy, that is, among the 20 per cent of the population not involved in traditional, subsistence agriculture. The International Monetary Fund survey (*Surveys of African Economies*, Vol. I [Washington, D.C.: I.M.F., 1968], p. 57) shows an increase in the monetary sector from 1959 to 1963/64 of 79.1 million CFA francs to 119.8 million CFA, or 40.7 million CFA, while the subsistence sector increased from 34.5 million CFA to 36.7 million CFA, or 2.2 million CFA. The difference, compensating for the inclusion of West Cameroon in the 1964/65 data, is an increase of about 51 per cent in the monetary sector as against an increase of only about 6 per cent in the subsistence sector. Hugon (see next note), incidentally, gives 99.1 million CFA as the 1959 figures, which suggests an even higher increase.

[8] Hugon, *Analyse du sous-développement en Afrique noire: L'exemple de l'économie du Cameroun* (Paris: Presses Universetaires de France, 1968), p. 314.

velopment plans, designated the First Five-Year Plan (1960–1965) and the Second Five-Year Plan (1965–1970).[9] The older twenty-year plan, substantially revised, remains the general framework for the two short-term plans. The first Five-Year Plan was produced and in some haste by a French research and planning group and, according to Hugon, without adequate preliminary study. Put together before unification, the first plan failed to take into consideration the entrance of West Cameroon into the total economy, and was hence somewhat unrealistic in its provisions. Without going into detail, it can be said that the results achieved under the first plan only partially corresponded to its stated aims. To be sure, in such areas as infrastructure (roads, railways, etc.) public education, health, and housing, the objectives of the plan were mostly met or even surpassed, and the gross industrial and infrastructural investments continued at a high rate during the period of its existence. But, as Hugon has pointed out, investment in the latter two areas tended to be largely uncontrolled and failed to correspond to the requirements of the plan itself. Moreover, and most seriously, very little progress was realized in the agricultural sector, one of the plan's key points of emphasis. Agricultural production, as compared to the rest of the economy, advanced at a rate of only 2.2 per cent per year. Withal, Hugon suggests that the First Five-Year Plan permitted the creation of structures necessary to the success of the Second; the 1960–1965 period was principally, to use Hugon's phrase, "a period of adaptation."

The Second Five-Year Plan, this time elaborated under

[9] The analysis of the results of the first plan rest principally on *ibid.,* pp. 249–254.

Cameroonian auspices, strove to remedy the defects and failures of the first.[10] Before an examination is made of several of this plan's specific goals, the problem of funding and cost needs to be considered briefly. The plan envisages a total investment of 165,000 million CFA (ca. $673 million), more than three times that scheduled for the first plan. Of the total, 45.6 per cent is to be devoted to increasing overall production, 35.1 per cent for infrastructural development, 15.8 per cent for "social equipment" (schools, hospitals, housing, etc.), and 3.5 per cent for administrative costs and studies. The main sources of funding are expected to be the federal budget (26.9 per cent), grants and loans from external sources (37.1 per cent), and private funds (36 per cent). It is hoped that over 50 per cent of the plan can be financed from purely Cameroonian sources. Whether these figures are realistic or not is a matter of opinion, but some doubts have already been expressed privately that the plan is "utopian" in its financing aspects, particularly since it specifically admits that up to 50 per cent will have to come from outside sources. Since most of Cameroon's development funding has thus far been provided on the basis of bilateral agreements, the possibility arises that these sources, espe-

[10] My discussion of the second plan rests principally on the following analyses and descriptions: *ibid.*, pp. 254–265; Daniel B. Masuke, "L'Elaboration du Premier Plan Fédéral du Développement," *Europe-France-Outremer*, XLIII, No. 436 (May 1966), 35–37; IMF, *op. cit.*, pp. 76–80; "Cameroon's 'Peasant' Plan," *West Africa*, Aug. 5, 1967, p. 1015. Text of the plan itself is contained in Ministry of Economic Affairs and the Plan, *Second Five-Year Economic and Social Development Plan, July, 1966–June, 1971* (Yaoundé: The Ministry, 1965).

cially France, either cannot or will not maintain their present rate of aid. The alternative is increased dependence upon multilateral and/or international aid and investment, but, as Paul Marc Henry, speaking of the continent as a whole, has warned, "the net result of this reorganization may well be a net decrease in the aggregate volume of aid received by Africa and not the expected increase." [11]

If the Second Five-Year Plan has any key aspects they undoubtedly lie in three areas: agricultural reform and reorganization, the prospects for industrialization, and *le grand projet,* the north-south railway axis.

AGRICULTURAL REFORM

The second plan, as did the first, sets as its goal the doubling of per capita income by 1980, which implies a growth rate for the GDP of about 5½ per cent per annum. The task, if the data are accurate, is an extraordinarily difficult one, particularly for the more than 80 per cent of the population still engaged in subsistence agriculture. The 8.6 per cent GDP growth rate cited by President Ahidjo in March 1969 conceals a disparity in the growth of the monetary sector of the economy (51 per cent between 1959 and 1964–65) as compared to that of the subsistence (agricultural) sector (6 per cent between 1959 and 1964–65). In any case, the second plan has been called the "Peasant Plan," since it puts specific emphasis on accelerating the commercialization of the agricultural sector and to redressing some of the imbalances within the

[11] Paul Marc Henry, "The United Nations and the Problem of African Development," *International Organization,* XVI, No. 2 (Spring 1962), 362.

system that stem from the gross disparities in income between wage earners and peasants.

The structures needed for the realization of these goals
already exist in part. The extent and growth of production
and marketing cooperatives have already been noted,
particularly those involving major export crops such as
cocoa, coffee, and the like. East Cameroon has presently
some 1,500 cooperatives, of which about 1,300 are financial
in nature. In addition to the cooperatives, five so-called
Agricultural Modernization Centers (SEMCENTRES) were
created by the government to coordinate development, research, and technical aid relating to the principal crops
grown in the five geographical areas served by the Centers.

In addition, federal agencies are to be created to carry
out the details of the rural programs, land reform—particularly in the area of communal landownership—is to be
carried out, and rural education projects are now under
way. Finally, the plan calls for the creation of regional
development societies, much like the "small landholders"
development authorities" in Rwanda and Malaysia, which
will combine plantations and agro-industrial complexes as
well as supervise the creation of rural development funds
to distribute agricultural credit.

A key facet of the agricultural part of the plan involves
the radical improvement of peasant export production
through the diversification of cash crops. The economy
already exports large amounts of cocoa, coffee, bananas,
woods, cotton, and the like; it is hoped to increase production of tea, rubber, and palm products. The need for
such diversification is particularly acute in West Cameroon, where a steady decline in banana production (the
state's leading export cash crop) has only been partially

offest by increases in the production of rubber, cocoa, palm oil, tea and pepper, and by the introduction of new banana varieties.[12]

The whole agricultural plan rests, however, upon an inherently unstable base; its projections assume relatively stable prices and markets for the country's principal export crops. The point has not been lost upon Cameroon's leaders, as *West Africa* magazine pointed out in an article dealing with the deterioration of the terms of trade between developed and underdeveloped economies:

[Ahidjo] told the EEC Commission in Brussels last month [July 1967]: "We are selling you hardly any more coffee and edible oils than we were in 1926. We are selling you less rice, vegetable-oils and cotton, and although you are buying more cocoa and bananas from us, it must be admitted that the increase in cocoa imports coincided with the disastrous price slump of 1965, and that the extra amounts of bananas that found their way to your markets did so often with enormous difficulty and at rock-bottom prices. We are selling to you at lower prices, and you to us at higher prices." [13]

How successful has the plan been in meeting its agricultural objectives? There are as yet no reliable data to warrant either jubilation or dismay. One authoritative source, the *Moniteur africain du commerce et de l'industrie,* reported that during the first six months of 1968, the value of Cameroonian exports increased faster than that of imports, a development attributable to the growth of agricultural exports and the reduction of imports in sectors now supplied by local produce. Thus, the govern-

[12] *Africa Research Bulletin* (Economic, Social, and Cultural series), July 15–Aug. 14, 1968, p. 1088.

[13] "Cameroon's 'Peasant' Plan," *loc. cit.*

ment was able to raise salaries in the private sector by 4 per cent to offset inflationary pressures that had been building up since 1961.[14] The fragility of the system, even given moderate success of its planning effort, was stressed by President Ahidjo during his report to the CNU congress in March 1969. It is a fascinating reminder of the extent to which agriculture controls the economies of most tropical countries, and of the effect of a fall in the world market price of a crucial commodity—cocoa—on one of the stronger and more highly diversified of such economic systems:

During the four years preceding reunification, the GDP, a good measure of national income, increased by 33 per cent. This result, remarkable by itself, would have been more so had not the international cocoa market collapsed in 1965.

At the same time, public expenditures increased by 62 per cent and bank obligations by 50 per cent.

The consequences were immediate:

–A budget deficit in East Cameroon for 1965/66;

–A Federal budget deficit for 1966/67;

–A large negative balance of trade in 1967;

–Rapid diminution of the State Treasury and of our foreign balances.[15]

By 1969 the international market price of cocoa had risen again, this time to new heights, and Cameroon was able to emerge from its economic doldrums. Despite efforts to prevent a recurrence of the 1965 disaster, the economy, tied as it is to agriculture and in particular to the export of commodities widely produced elsewhere and still poorly

[14] Cited in *Africa Research Bulletin* (Economic, etc. series), April 15–May 14, 1969, p. 1335.

[15] *L'Unité* (Yaoundé), March 1969, p. 5.

regulated on the international market, continues to be highly vulnerable in—paradoxically—its strongest sector.

PROSPECTS FOR INDUSTRIALIZATION

Whatever else is said of the industrialization potential of the federation, two facts stand out at once: (1) that the greatest possibilities lie in East Cameroon and (2) that major industrial projects designed to produce items for export are out of the question for the federation in the foreseeable future. The latter is one of the conclusions reached in a 1960 report prepared by a French firm assigned to study the possibilities for industrial development in Cameroon.[16] Given the high cost of capital and construction, the poverty in the infrastructure, the limited natural resources of the federation, and the difficulties involved in trying to compete in markets dominated by industrial nations, only limited industrial expansion can have any economic justification.[17] The consequences of this conclusion are obvious. According to the report, Cameroon industrial development must be directed toward the creation of industry, most of it on a fairly small scale, designed to serve local markets. Some dozen or so enterprises, including meat canning, flour milling and biscuit production, and the manufacture of matches, tennis shoes, soap, plywood, cement, and plastics would have utility within the range of the Cameroon's limited economic potential.

The Edéa aluminum plant, one of two exceptions to the

[16] Société d'Etudes pour le Développement Economique et Social, *Rapport sur les possibilités de développement industriel du Cameroun* (Paris: La Société, 1960), p. 2.

[17] Hugon agrees: see *op. cit.*, pp. 104–122.

"no large industry" rule, was constructed, it will be re-called, to take advantage of the potential for extremely cheap hydroelectric power available at the Edéa falls on the Sanaga River. Its expansion seems to be economically unprofitable for the moment, principally because bauxite must still be brought to Edéa from outside sources and because the world market for aluminum is already quite inelastic. The report referred to does not discourage ex-pansion of the existing facilities for the manufacture of aluminum utensils made from Edéa ingots, but it stresses that economic reality must dictate that such production be directed to internal, rather than external, markets. Finally, a large area of uncertainty exists with regard to the ex-ploitation of the extensive bauxite deposits at Martap near Tibati. These ores will be available only when the Douala-Chad railway is extended the more than 400 miles north from Yaoundé to reach the deposits; this extension may not be completed until at least 1975, at the rate construc-tion was proceeding in 1969. Further, the unpredictable state of the world aluminum market in 1975 and the extremely high initial costs of transportation on the rail-way pose still other problems. As a hedge against some of these problems, the government, in 1970, signed an agree-ment with French and German aluminum interests to form a company to undertake further study of the Martap deposits and, possibly, to exploit them at a later date.

The other exception is the textile industry which hopes, during 1970/71, to achieve a gross turnover of about 8,000 million CFA (ca. $32.6 m.) per year, of which perhaps half is destined for export, principally in the Central African Customs and Economic Union (UDEAC) region. Three firms are presently involved: one French, two

French-Cameroonian, of which the largest is SAFRITEX (Société Africaine des Textiles), engaged in the manufacture of over one million cotton items a year.

THE NORTH-SOUTH RAILWAY AXIS [18]

Since the German protectorate, extension of Cameroon's railway system northward to the Chad Basin has been an object of great interest. In 1930, the French administration undertook a survey of the prolongation of the Douala-Yaoundé line north to Ngaoundéré and thence to the Chad territory itself. The project lay dormant, but not forgotten, until 1945, when interest was revived by the French, and in 1948 a series of studies was begun to determine the economic, political, and financial feasibility of a Douala-Chad railway. With independence, the Cameroun Republic pushed the project even further, to the extent of adopting the studies made by a governmental agency charged with examining the project and seeking international financing for it. The railway now represents the single most important development project in the country. By 1963, the Cameroon government had obtained financing in the amount of $36.3 million. From a consortium of French, American, and Common Market sources to complete the first—i.e. Yaoundé-Bélabo—section. The second section, from Belabo to Ngaoundéré, a distance of 218 (of the total 394) miles, is being financed by the same

[18] For additional information see "Le Transcamerounais," *Europe-France-Outremer,* XLIII No. 436 (May 1966), pp. 25–29; "By Train to Chad?" *West Africa,* May 18, 1968, p. 582; Commissariat Général à l'Information, *Le Chemin de Fer Transcamerounais* (Yaoundé: n.d.), in both English and French; *Afrique 69/70* (Paris: Société Africaine Presse Associée, 1969), pp. 151–154.

sources at an approximate cost of $44.9 million. The Yaoundé-Bélabo section was to have been finished during the first months of 1968. In fact, by May 1968, it had only got to Nanga-Eboko, 177 kilometers from Yaoundé; Bélabo is 124 kilometers further. The original projection was that the railway would reach Ngaoundéré on June 1, 1970, with the second section (Bélabo-Ngaoundéré) scheduled to be completed in the same time (40 months) as the first. The project was begun in October 1964, and it took 43 months to go the first 177 kilometers; at that rate, it would take another 7.1 years for the railway to get to Ngaoundéré. That puts its completion sometime into 1975, or at best, late 1974, providing construction can be speeded up on what is admittedly the harder section to build (the road must climb 1,611 feet to Ngaoundéré from Bélabo). Not even the most optimistic private projections envision completion of the project earlier than mid-1974, or four years later than planned. The most optimistic *public* projections are 1972 or 1973.[19]

The original plans called only for an extension of the then existing Douala-Yaoundé line to Ngaoundéré, but studies have been under way for two eventual branches, one from about midway between Yaoundé and Ngaoundéré eastward to Bangui, the capital of the Central African Republic, and the other, a northeastern extension from Ngaoundéré to Fort Archambault in Chad. Fort Archambault connects with Fort Lamy, the capital of Chad, by way of the Chari River, a distance of 312 miles.

The political and economic ramifications of the project as a whole are far-reaching for Cameroon and for the Chad–Central African Republic area of the Lake Chad

[19] These projections were reported by R. W. Apple, New York *Times,* June 14, 1969.

Basin. (1) The Douala-Chad railway would provide a new
and profitable means of access to the sea for an area of
more than 193,000 square miles with over 2,700,000 inhabitants. The area in question has heretofore had only
limited and difficult access to seaports. The north Cameroon–Fort Lamy areas have been served by the Benue
River from Garoua and by the Nigerian railway system's
extension to Northern Nigeria and alternatively (for Chad)
by the difficult connections overland and by river south
to Brazzaville. The new rail line would shorten the distance to the sea, cut the time required to move goods in
and out of the area, and eventually lower the cost of
transportation from the region by more than two-thirds.
(2) The completion of the project is one of the vital requirements for the realization of the Cameroonian plan;
without it, the development of the Cameroon north becomes almost impossible. In particular, as was noted, it
will permit access to the Martap-Tibati bauxites, impossible in any other way. (3) The railway opens one door
to a closer integration of the equatorial African group, to
which Cameroon now belongs through the Central African
Customs and Economic Union (UDEAC). (4) It should
help redress the old regional economic imbalance between
the Cameroon north and south; the north, until the railway began heading in that direction, has had to rely on
the seasonal rise of the Benué at Garoua and poor dirt
roads to move its products south.

External Relations

WITH OTHER AFRICAN STATES

In general, the federation pursues its relations with
other African states within the framework of its membership in the Organization of African Unity (OAU), the

Organisation Commune Africaine et Malagache (OCAM, Joint African and Malagasy Organization), and the Union Douanière et Economique de l'Afrique Centrale (UDEAC, Central African Customs and Economic Union). Cameroonian commitment to the OCAM is undoubtedly grounded both in the members' common ties to France— and the European Common Market—and in the fact that the looseness of the organization permits each member state a wide latitude of individual freedom of action. In general, Cameroonian foreign policy in the African arena has few specific objectives and has been directed to such vague goals as broader economic, social, and political cooperation between all African states, to increasing cooperation with the European Economic Community as an associate member, and to such indefinite policies as support of the United Nations' effort in the Congo, condemnation of racism in South Africa and the Rhodesias, and opposition to nuclear testing in the Sahara.

Ghana, until the coup that overthrew the regime of President Nkrumah in February 1966, and Guinea, until recently, have constituted special problems for Cameroon. Both Ghana and Guinea played host to the exiled UPC leadership, and the Ahidjo government was regularly the target of denunciation from Accra and Conakry. In January 1962, Ghana decided to recognize the federation and sought to establish diplomatic relations with Cameroon. Despite its overt attempts at friendliness, the Ghanaian government secretly continued to train and equip UPC militants for subversion in Cameroon, a fact which was known in Yaoundé but did not become public knowledge until after the Nkrumah regime was overthrown. Since then, relations between the two countries have been good, though the expected exchange of diplomatic missions never took place. In any case, Ghana no longer supports the UPC militants and has, in fact, warned those of the old UPC cadre left in the country (like Martin Tchapchet) to refrain from any sort of political activity or be deported. Even after Nkrumah's downfall Guinea continued to provide some haven for the UPC exiles; but it was in 1964, after that support began to diminish, that relations between the two countries began to improve.

More recently, the Nigerian civil war posed some difficult problems for the Federation. The former secessionist state of Biafra lay directly west of West Cameroon, and during the height of the fighting, thousands of refugees from Biafra sought shelter in the adjoining Cameroon areas. Between 1968 and 1970, perhaps as many as 25,000 Ibos fled to West Cameroon; most of them were sheltered in refugee camps maintained by the Cameroon government. To complicate matters, a good many Ibos resident in West Cameroon, as well as many West Cameroonians, made no secret of their sympathies for the Biafran cause. Throughout the period of the civil war the Cameroon government maintained a posture of support for the Nigerian central government, but sought in various ways to mediate the dispute. The Cameroon government was involved in efforts by the United Nations, the Organization of African Unity, and some western governments, to bring the conflict to an end. When the civil war did end early in 1970, Cameroon offered its good offices in reconciling the Nigerian government with those African states—such as the Ivory Coast and Gabon—who had recognized and openly helped the Biafrans. One result of Cameroon's support for Nigeria during the civil war was an official visit to Cameroon by the Nigerian Head of State, Maj. Gen. Yakubu Gowon, during which a long-standing dispute over the Cameroon-Nigerian frontier in the coastal Rio de Rey area was settled amicably.

WITH NON-AFRICAN STATES

By 1971 forty-five states had accredited missions to Yaoundé, of which twenty-three had established embassies in the federal capital. In addition, the Vatican and the Sovereign Order of Malta had resident representatives, and nine countries had opened consulates variously in Yaoundé, Douala, or Buea. Cameroon is an associate member of the Common Market, and almost all of its aid from abroad comes from Western sources. Consequently, almost all its foreign relations, as reflected in the countries represented in Yaoundé, have tended to be with Europe, North America, and nations conventionally associated with the non-Communist world. The first step to a wider series of contacts was taken in September 1962, when a good-will mission headed by Victor Kanga, Federal Minister of National Economy, visited Warsaw, Prague, and Moscow, as well as Stockholm and Copenhagen. Shortly thereafter, the Soviet Union opened an embassy in Yaoundé.

Until April 1971, the presence of a Nationalist Chinese Embassy in Yaoundé bore special witness to the Ahidjo regime's hostility to the government of mainland China, which had been for many years an active financial supporter of and host to the "external" UPC. On April 2, 1971, the Cameroon government reversed its position and agreed to an exchange of diplomatic personnel with Communist China. The move was explained partially as a response to changing international conditions (an increasing number of African states had done likewise) and partially in light of the fact that the Communist Chinese had ceased their support of the UPC. Informed sources suggested yet another motive: the presence of a large Communist Chinese mission in Equatorial Guinea, next door, had made it seem politic that they be invited to Yaoundé, if only because they could be more closely watched that way.

In all, the Federal Republic's contacts with non-African states have not been extensive, a fact due primarily to the high cost of spreading diplomatic posts to an increasingly large community of nations. Its primary contacts continue to be with the larger states of Europe, the United States, the United Nations, and its immediate African neighbors.

WITH THE UNITED NATIONS

Cameroon became a member of the United Nations in 1960 and maintains a permanent mission in New York. Within the General Assembly the Federal Republic's representatives orient themselves according to the postures developed by the "African caucus," and more particularly to the positions of the OCAM group at the UN. At least insofar as Cameroon is concerned, the relationship with the OCAM (formerly the "Brazzaville") group has been a salutary one. During the debates in the spring of 1961, the Brazzaville group supported en bloc Cameroon's demand for a new plebiscite in the Northern British Cameroons.

The Federal Republic, on the whole, gives only qualified support to the United Nations, but it maintains its membership in various UN agencies such as the Economic

Commission for Africa, the Commission for Technical Cooperation in Africa South of the Sahara, the World Health Organization, the International Labor Organization, the Food and Agriculture Organization, and the United Nations Educational, Scientific, and Cultural Organization.

CHAPTER 5

Ten Years of Federation: Looking Back—and Ahead

On October 1, 1971, the Cameroon Federal Republic marks its first decade of existence. Amid much recalling with pride and much looking ahead with optimism and confidence, the occasion could be regarded also as a time of personal triumph for President Ahidjo, under whose guidance the federation has survived ten years. Rhetoric aside, what is unusual about the occasion is that the praise is largely merited and the pride and confidence mostly justified. A simple look at Cameroon's overall record of political stability and social and economic growth since 1961, compared to that of its African neighbors, is sufficient to make the point.

Between 1961 and 1971 no fewer than twenty-nine African governments were overthrown: three in 1963, two in 1964, five in 1965, seven in 1966, five in 1967, three in 1968, four in 1969, and none in 1970. That comes to the distressing average of about three per year. To reinforce the point, Cameroon's immediate neighbors have all experienced serious internal difficulties or coups: Gabon's attempted military coup in 1964, suppressed by French paratroops; Congo/Brazzaville has had two coups (1966 and 1968); the Central African Republic had one (1966); since 1968 Chad has been fighting what it admitted in 1970 to be an open rebellion; and, of course, Nigeria experienced almost uninterrupted internal conflict between 1964 and the beginning of 1970.

The comparative economic data show Cameroon in an equally favorable light. Again, the simplest, even crudest, comparative indices tell the story. For example, the International Monetary Fund reported that in 1966 the gross domestic product of the five-country UDEAC area (Cameroon, Chad. C.A.R., Congo/Brazzaville, and Gabon) was estimated at about $1.4 billion, "almost half of which was generated in Cameroon." [1] The annual growth rate of the Cameroon economy has been estimated (at current prices between 1960 and 1966) as 7–8 per cent; this compares favorably with that of Gabon (9.5 per cent) and of the Ivory Coast (ca. 11 per cent).[2]

Above all, however, it is the country's internal political picture that provides the best reasons for Cameroonian self-congratulation. At independence, in 1960, the government of the Cameroun Republic was under violent attack from the political dissidents who had been fomenting rebellion in the western and southwestern parts of the territory since 1955. On January 1, 1960, the day of independence itself, the rebels attacked vital points in Douala and in various other towns. A large French military contingent (perhaps upward of 2,000 men) was in the field attempting to suppress the rebels. Abroad, the UPC and its several host governments redoubled their efforts to topple the government of Prime Minister Ahidjo, described as a "lackey of imperialism," and a *fantoche*

[1] International Monetary Fund, *Surveys of African Economies* Vol. I (Washington, D.C.: I.M.F., 1968), p. 4.

[2] *Africa Research Bulletin* (Economic, Financial, and Technical Series) various issues, 1968–1969.

(puppet) of the French. There is no need to recount the story told earlier in greater detail; it is enough to recall that a combination of vigorous military initiatives and astute political moves by the government virtually eliminated the internal aspects of the rebellion by the end of 1962. Thereafter, Osende Afana and Ernest Ouandié could do little more than lead the small bands of UPC *maquis* remaining in the country on occasional harassing raids.

Ahidjo and his colleagues first outflanked their opponents by making the *maquis* militarily costly and politically unprofitable, and then disarmed them by co-opting the leaders of the internal UPC into the governing elite. Reunification, accomplished in 1961, proved immensely popular and helped to increase general support for the regime. By 1962, Ahidjo could move against the remaining legal opposition in East Cameroon by temporarily removing its four principal leaders from the political arena. Thereafter, the business of internal political consolidation could move much more smoothly, and by 1966, under firm but insistent pressures, even what was left of West Cameroonian separatist politicians had agreed to join the single national party, the CNU. Let me stress again that, in my opinion, it was Ahidjo's tactics that made the difference in the final analysis. He treated his opponents firmly, sometimes harshly, but made sure that even his bitterest enemies had both the chance of joining his side and of actively sharing in the perquisites of rule. That he was never vindictive is to his credit: Mbida was repeatedly offered various portfolios, Okala came out of prison to become an ambassador, and several former UPC leaders have taken high and well-paying jobs in government. The

style of the regime appears to have been actively reconciliationist, pragmatic, and tactically consistent.

In sum, then, the ability of the Ahidjo regime to include almost all the most important politically active
people in the country—or at least to secure their acqui-
escence—coupled with visible measures of social and economic progress, plus the operation of what appears to be
a relatively honest governmental system have all helped
maintain political peace in Cameroon when countries elsewhere in Africa have been less fortunate.

Looking back at what has gone right or wrong with a
country is a fairly easy thing to do: of all sight, hindsight
is clearest. Certainly, in 1960, a restrained pessimism about
Cameroon's future would have been the better part of
predictive valor. (Indeed, given the fact that since 1960,
only a handful of African states have escaped internal
political upheaval, pessimism about the political future of
Cameroon would have been the safer bet.) What of the
future, now, more than ten years later?

In other African states, the military have shown a
disposition to intervene when, (*a*) civilian rulers have
proved manifestly unable or unwilling to prevent (at
least, so it appeared to the military) the imminent political,
economic, or social collapse of the system, or all three;
(*b*) when the regime appears to threaten the status, or
even the very survival of the military establishment (by
the creation of competing military or paramilitary elites,
for example); (*c*) when the military thinks it can do a
better job of running the country and gets up enough
nerve to try to do so; or (*d*) when two or all three of
these circumstances exist simultaneously. By late 1970,
none of these conditions appeared to exist in Cameroon.

Certainly, the regime did not make the mistake (as was the case in Mali, Ghana, or Congo/Brazzaville) of seeming to undermine the military by attempting to create a paramilitary arm of the government. Further, relative political peace prevailed and visible economic and social progress was being made. Moreover, it seemed unlikely that the military could do a better job of governing than the group headed by President Ahidjo and the two regional Prime Ministers. Of course, the unexpected can always occur, but at least military intervention seems remote and unlikely unless the situation changes drastically for the worse and one or more of the above situations makes its appearance.

On the economic front the situation looks quite hopeful. Cameroon has become an attractive place in which to invest, and international donors and lenders of development capital have shown increasing disposition to make Cameroon a beneficiary of their attentions. Though life has become somewhat expensive for the average Cameroonian (inflation, for example, has devalued the 8 per cent GDP growth rate to a real value of about 3.5 per cent), food and consumer goods are relatively plentiful, and the development of the internal road and rail system has spurred the growth of commercial agriculture of all kinds. The present agricultural program, financed largely by the World Bank, the International Development Association, and the Common Market, envisages an expansion of the total area under cultivation to 33,100,000 hectares, or an increase of 48 per cent by the end of 1974.[3] Modest

[3] In 1960/61, an estimated 828,000 hectares grew some 2,377,000 metric tons of crops mainly for domestic (Eastern) consumption; in 1964/65 some 3,511,000 hectares in the federation were under cultivation, with a yield of ca. 2,616,000 metric tons of crops. A

increments continue to be registered in Cameroon's industrial plant, and despite occasional balance of payments problems (owing principally to fluctuations in the world market prices for its prime export crops, and increases of imports over exports), the country may in fact become the industrial center for the equatorial region, a development favored by the UDEAC arrangements. Withal, the point to be made is that none of Cameroon's economic problems seems either excessively vexing or insoluble. The country's economy is basically strong, and with judicious planning and management, has considerable room for expansion.

Some of the most difficult questions for the future lie, most probably, in the social realm. It is a fact that the country's ethnic groups are still relatively malintegrated. The problems posed by the old north-south ethnic antagonisms, by the expansion of the dynamic Bamiléké, by unemployment and poverty in the main towns—to mention only a few areas of social tension—have yet to be directly confronted. That the old tensions surface every so often with explosive violence has been noted. But again, here as elsewhere, the prospects are relatively good. It may take decades to make inroads into these problems, but with internal peace, steady economic growth, and responsible leadership, none of them will become so acute as to threaten the political and social fabric of the country.

We come, finally, to the most imponderable question, that of the succession to the present leadership. Here, perhaps, lies the greatest potential danger to the Cameroon's

---

similar increase in both area and yield for export crops was registered during the same period (I.M.F., *op. cit.,* pp. 60–63).

political system. It is a melancholy fact that in only a handful of cases has African post-independence leadership succession been arranged peacefully and according to constitutional rules. It is not that the rules were not there—in every country experiencing a violent seizure of power, constitutional provision for peaceful transition existed—but that they either were not observed or failed to exert much influence in succession crises. Cameroon is perhaps lucky to have a young president, but youth has not proven a deterrent to coups in other situations. What is important is (a) whether Ahidjo has in fact sought to groom a possible successor (or successors); [4] (b) whether the rules for succession are sufficiently respected by likely claimants to power; (c) whether the system will be sufficiently flexible to withstand a succession crisis when (or if) it occurs and; (d) whether a whole generation of leaders—who came up with Ahidjo—will be willing to relinquish power when and if the occasion arises. No answers, even tentative ones, are possible to these questions; it is, however, demonstrably a fact that a new, post-independence Cameroonian elite is waiting, both in the wings and within the establishment. Whether the ruling elite will have the wisdom to provide for peaceful transition, and then give way gracefully, remains to be seen. I hope that in this, as elsewhere in the system, an optimistic forecast is justified.

[4] Mr. Solomon Tandeng Muna, former West Cameroon Prime Minister, became federal Vice President following the March 1970 presidential elections. Whether this represents the anointing of a successor (*constitutionally* it does, of course) is another question. (Muna was also reappointed Prime Minister of West Cameroon.)

Bibliography

Until about 1963, the English-language literature on Cameroon was primarily the work of social scientists devoted to ethnographic and sociological matters, or of administrators, travelers and missionaries with interests in the area. With one conspicuous exception, such literature dealt almost exculsively with the former British Cameroons, now West Cameroon. The exception is Harry Rudin's classic *Germans in the Cameroons,* first published by Yale University Press in 1938, and reprinted in 1969 by Archon Books. It was the first, and remains the best, study of the German period, as well as one of the finest case studies of colonialism in print. (More recently, in 1960, an anthology edited by Helmuth Stoecker, based on colonial archival material located in East Germany, was published in German.) Of particular importance among the pre-1963 literature is the work of Edwin and Shirley Ardener, W. A. Warmington, Phyllis Kaberry, E. M. Chilver, and P. R. Kuczinski. Three American anthropologists, Robert and Pat Ritzenthaler and Paul Gebauer (who had served thirty years as a missionary in Bamenda), published monographs in 1962 and 1964 dealing with West Cameroon life.

In 1963 the first full-length political study of Cameroon, David Gardinier's *Cameroon: United Nations Challenge to French Policy,* was published. Gardinier, also a former student of Rudin's, dealt with the effects, both domestic and international, of the French trusteeship over what was, until 1960, the French Cameroun. Also, my section on *The Cameroun* in Gwendolen Carter's *Five African States* (the basis of the present revised study), which dealt with general political, social, and economic problems, was published in 1963. My own full-scale study of the political evolution of both Cameroons territories, *The Cameroons from Mandate to Independence,* followed in 1964. My study of Cameroonian political parties, in Coleman and Rosberg's collection (see below) appeared in 1964. More recent work, Claude Welch's Cameroons chapters in his *Dream of Unity* (1966), Edwin Ardener's section in Hazelwood's *African Integration and Disintegration* (1967), and Willard Johnson's *The Cameroon Federation* (1970) deal with the processes, background, and effects of the unification of Cameroon. All three are excellent and highly informative. Guy de Lusignan's *French-Speaking Africa Since Independence* (1969) contains a section on Cameroon, but this is, unfortunately, marred by frequent errors of fact. Of much higher quality is Edward Mortimer's *France and the Africans* (1969), in which aspects of Cameroon's political history are discussed in some detail. Mortimer profited from the opportunity to use Dr. L.-P. Aujoulat's papers and notes.

Recently, Cameroon-born scholars have begun to publish books and articles on their country and its affairs. Leading the way was the excellent bilingual review, *Abbia,* edited by Bernard Fonlon, which printed not only articles by such contemporary Cameroonian intellectuals as B. J. Fouda, J. A. Kisob, M. Towa, the Reverend E. Mveng, and E. Mohammadou, but also thoughtful and sometimes provocative pieces by Fonlon himself. Father Mveng, probably the best of the Cameroonian historians, published his *Histoire du Cameroun* in 1963; unfortunately, he only devotes twenty of his 533 pages to the period 1945–1961, so discussion of that period must be sought in the various work by Ardener, Gardinier, Welch, Johnson, and myself. Of particular note, too, is the work of Eldridge Mohammadou, a research associate of the Federal Linguistic and Cultural Center in Yaoundé. Mohammadou's several historical studies of northern Cameroonian emirates, lamidates, sultanates, and sheikhdoms, printed in

Abbia, constitute in their ensemble the best history of that area yet written. The Abbé Thomas Ketchoua's *Contribution à l'histoire du Cameroun* (a collection of primary documents) and Enoch K. Kwayeb's *Les Institutions de droit public du pays Bamiléké* (a study of traditional and modern legal institutions among the Bamiléké) are also worthy of note. A recent book by a young Cameroonian lawyer, H. N. A. Enonchong, *Cameroon Constitutional Law* (1967), provides not only a constitutional history of the country, but a detailed examination of its federal law as well. Finally, the late Peter M. Kale's *Political Evolution in the Cameroons* is noteworthy as one of the few political studies done by a Cameroonian.

The general literature on the French Cameroun, now East Cameroon, is considerably more extensive, but save for a few articles in English and the political studies noted above, is almost entirely in French. Most of these materials deal with nonpolitical matters: formal studies of administrative institutions, French government-inspired praise of the French colonial effort, economic reports, and a variety of articles in such periodicals as *Europe-France-Outremer* (which has devoted several issues since 1959 to Cameroon), *Marchés tropicaux et méditerranéens, Jeune Afrique* (published in Algiers), and *Afrique Nouvelle* (published in Dakar). In any case, Cameroon materials in French are even harder to find than those in English. Only the libraries of universities offering extensive study of African culture and politics are likely to have more than an unrepresentative sampling.

Undoubtedly, the best of the French-language material is that dealing with Cameroonian anthropology and ethnography. In this connection, two of the few recent French works on Cameroon should be mentioned; both deal with the Bamiléké: Claude Tardits' *Les Bamiléké de l'ouest Cameroun* (1960), and J. Hurault's *La Structure sociale des Bamiléké* (1962) give, together, what is probably the best statement of the sociodemographic roots of *le problème Bamiléké.* The first non-Cameroonian commentary on an analysis of Cameroon's economy recently appeared in the form of Philippe Hugon's *Analyse du sous-développement en Afrique noire: l'exemple de l'économie du Cameroun* (1968). Hugon, a French economist, taught at the Federal University in Yaoundé. Data on the French Cameroun before 1960 can be found in the French government's annual reports to the United Nations Trusteeship Council; these volumes, however, go up only to 1957 and are unwieldy and often uninformative. A full set of the French reports, and of the reports on the British Cameroons, may be found at the Hammarskjold Library at United Nations headquarters in New York.

A surprisingly extensive German-language literature on Cameroon was published, not only during the period of the German protectorate, but during the interwar years when Nazi Germany launched a massive propaganda campaign for the return of its former colonies. Much of this material reflects the political purposes for which it was published, but in it can be found valuable accounts of settler life in the Kamerun, of explorations, and of economic and social conditions both during and after the protectorate. Again, unfortunately, these works are not generally available. Probably the largest and best collection of German works on the Kamerun in the United States can be found in the New York Public Library. Currently, only one reliable account of Cameroon politics exists in German; Franz Ansprenger in his *Politik im Schwarzen Afrika* (1961) devotes two chapters to the Kamerun's political development. Stoecker's collection of articles on the protectorate period was mentioned above.

The bibliography that follows is, by necessity, a highly selective one. A much more extensive bibliography, including a wide range of official documents and publications, may be found in my book, *The Cameroons from Mandate to Independence*. Johnson's book, *The Cameroon Federation*, also has a detailed bibliography. For a fuller survey of official publications, the Library of Congress' *Official Publications of French Equatorial Africa, French Cameroons, and Togo, 1946–1958* (Washington D.C., 1964), should be consulted. George Horner and I put together a bibliography of "Pre and Post-Independence Newspapers in Cameroons," in *Africana Newsletter* (later *Bulletin of the African Studies Association*) I, No. 2 (1963); my collection of Cameroonian political ephemera is catalogued in *Africana Newsletter,* I, No. 3 (1963), and is available on microfilm in the collection of the Cooperative Africana Microfilm Project (CAMP), currently available through the Center for Research Libraries, Chicago, Ill.

Books, Monographs, and Sections in Books

Ahidjo, Ahmadou. *Contributions à la construction nationale.* Paris: Présence Africaine, 1964. 137 pp. Text of President Ahidjo's report to the 1962 Union Camerounaise congress at Maroua.

Ansprenger, Franz. *Politik im Schwarzen Afrika: Die modernen politische Bewegungen im Afrika französischer Prägung.* Cologne and Opladen: Westdeutscher Verlag for the Deutsche Afrika-Gesellschaft e.u. Bonn, 1961. 516 pp. See headnote.

Ardener, Edwin. *Coastal Bantu of the Cameroons.* London: International African Institute, 1956. 116 pp. Ardener served as government anthropologist in West Cameroon from 1952 to 1961. The book embodies the essentials of the existing literature (in English, French, and Douala) and of thorough field research conducted by the author and his wife.

——, Shirley Ardener, and Alan Warmington. *Plantation and Village in the Cameroons.* London: Oxford University Press for the Nigerian Institute of Social and Economic Research, 1960. 435 pp. A socioeconomic ecology of the

Southern Cameroons, with particular emphasis on labor problems of the Cameroons Development Corporation.

Baeschlin-Raspail, Béat Chistophe. *Ahmadou Ahidjo, pionnier de l'Afrique moderne.* Printed in Monaco, 1968, distributed in Yaoundé by the Information Ministry of Cameroon. 119 pp. An officially-commissioned biography, published on the occasion of the tenth anniversary of President Ahidjo's rule.

Billard, Pierre. *Le Cameroun Fédéral.* 2 vols. Lyon: Imprimerie des Beaux-arts, 1968. Vol. 1 deals with Cameroon's physical geography; Vol. 2, dealing with "Human and Economic Geography" is flawed by considerable factual error.

Bouchaud, Joseph, *La Côte du Cameroun dans l'histoire et la cartographie des origines à l'annexion allemande.* Mémoires de l'Institut Français de l'Afrique Noire (IFAN) Centre du Cameroun: Histoire, No. 5. Yaoundé: IFAN Centre du Cameroun, 1952. 212 pp. Precolonial history of the Cameroun coast, pieced together from a remarkable variety of sources.

Buell, Raymond Leslie. *The Native Problem in Africa.* Vol. II. New York: Macmillan, 1928. 1049 pp. Part IV details the writer's eyewitness findings in the Cameroun mandate. Buell, an American professor, caused a great stir with the two-volume work.

Cameroon National Union, Political Bureau. *Ahmadou Ahidjo, par lui-même.* Printed in Monaco, 1968, distributed in Yaoundé by the CNU. 102 pp. An official biography and a selection from President Ahidjo's speeches, issued on the occasion of the tenth anniversary of his rule.

———. *The Political Philosophy of Ahmadou Ahidjo.* Yaoundé: CNU, 1968. 122 pp. An official statement, written anonymously, of President Ahidjo's philosophy, as culled from his speeches. Issued on the occasion of the tenth anniversary of his rule.

Chilver, E. M. "Native Administration in the West Central Cameroons, 1902–54." In Kenneth Robinson and Frederick Madden, eds., *Essays in Imperial Government*, pp. 201–246. London: Oxford University Press, 1963.

——. "Paramountcy and Protection in the Cameroons: The Bali and the Germans, 1889–1913." In R. Prosser and W. R. Louis, eds., *Britain and Germany in Africa: Imperial Rivalry and Colonial Rule*, pp. 479–511. New Haven: Yale University Press, 1967.

de Lusignan, Guy. *French-Speaking Africa Since Independence*. London: Pall Mall, 1969. See headnote.

Dugast, I[delette]. *Inventaire ethnique du Sud-Cameroun*. Mémoires de l'IFAN Centre du Cameroun: Populations, No. 1. Yaoundé: IFAN Centre du Cameroun, 1949. 139 pp. The only comprehensive work on the ethnic composition of the southern part of the East Cameroun. It is dated but still extremely valuable.

Enonchong, H. N. A. *Cameroon Constitutional Law*. Yaoundé: Centre d'Edition et de Production de Manuels et d'Auxiliaires de l'Enseignement, 1967. 314 pp. See headnote.

Gardinier, David E. "The British in the Cameroons, 1919–1939." In R. Prosser and W. R. Louis, eds., *Britain and Germany in Africa: Imperial Rivalry and Colonial Rule*, pp. 413–555. New Haven: Yale University Press, 1967.

Gebauer, Paul. *Spider Divination in the Cameroons*. Publications in Anthropology, No. 10. Milwaukee, Wis.: Milwaukee Public Museum, 1964. 157 pp. Rev. Gebauer, for thirty years a Baptist missionary in West Cameroon, has provided a fascinating account of a system of divination that uses the trapdoor spider and sets of precisely incised leaves.

Gonidec, P[ierre] F. *La République fédérale du Cameroun*. Paris: Berger-Levrault, 1969. 88 pp. Short but useful introduction to Cameroonian institutions and politics.

Green, Reginald Herbold. "The Economy of the Federal Republic of Cameroon." In P[eter] Robson and D[avid] A.

Lurie, eds., *The Economies of Africa,* pp. 236–286. London: George Allen and Unwin, 1969. The data are slightly dated, but this is an excellent structural analysis.

Hugon, Philippe. *Analyse du sous-développement en Afrique noire: L'exemple de l'économie du Cameroun.* Paris: Presses Universitaires de France, 1968. 325 pp. See headnote.

Hurault, J. *La Structure sociale des Bamiléké.* Paris: Mouton, 1962. 133 pp., and large fold-out map of Foumban-Bafoussam. Highly detailed, well-written study.

Johnson, Willard R. *The Cameroon Federation: Political Integration in a Fragmentary Society.* Princeton, N.J.: Princeton University Press, 1970.

———. "The Cameroon Federation: Political Union Between English-Speaking and French-Speaking Africa." In William H. Lewis, ed., *French-speaking Africa: The Search for Identity,* pp. 205–220. New York: Walker, 1965.

Kaberry, Phyllis M. *Women of the Grassfields.* Colonial Research, No. 14 London: H.M. Stationery Office, 1952. 220 pp. Although it focuses on the position of women in Bamenda, this excellent study offers a readable account of social and political organization among the grasslands tribes.

Kale, P[eter] M. *Political Evolution in the Cameroons.* Buea: West Cameroon Government Printer, 1968. 93 pp. The author became involved in West Cameroonian politics in the early 1940's, and the book includes his recollections of the more important political events, personalities, and issues.

Kanga, Victor Jean-Claude. *Le Droit coutumier Bamiléké au contact avec des droits européens.* Yaoundé: Etat du Cameroun, 1959.

Ketchoua, (l'Abbé) Thomas. *Contribution à l'histoire du Cameroun de 450 avant Jésus-Christ à nos jours.* Yaoundé: probably published under the auspices of the Catholic weekly, *L'Effort camerounais,* ca. 1962 or 1963.

Kuczinski, P. R. *The Cameroons and Togoland: A Demo-*

graphic Study. London: Oxford University Press, 1939. 579 pp.

Kwayeb, Enoch Katte. *Les Institutions de droit public du pays Bamiléké (Cameroun): Evolution et régime actuel.* Paris: R. Pichon and R. Durand-Auzias, Librairie Generale de Droit et de Jurisprudence, 1960. See headnote.

Lembezat, Bertrand. *Kirdi, les populations paiennes du nord-Cameroun.* Mémoires de l'IFAN Centre du Cameroun: Populations, No. 3. Yaoundé: IFAN Centre du Cameroun, 1950. 101 pp. Still the standard work on the animist tribes of the Cameroun north, it complements the work of Jean-Paul Lebeuf in Chad.

Le Vine, Victor T. "Cameroon (1955–1962)." In Doris M. Condit and Bert H. Cooper, eds., *Challange and Response in Internal Conflict,* III, 239–267. Washington, D.C.: American University, Center for Research in Social Systems, 1968.

———. *The Cameroons from Mandate to Independence.* Berkeley and Los Angeles: University of California Press, 1964. 320 pp. See headnote. French translation, *Le Cameroun.* Paris: Editions Nouveaux Horizons, 1970.

———. "Political Parties in the Cameroons." In James S. Coleman and Carl G. Rosberg, eds., *Political Parties and National Integration in Tropical Africa,* pp. 132–184. Berkeley: University of California Press, 1964.

———, and Henri M'Ballah. "[Education in the] Federal Republic of Cameroon." In Helen Kitchen, ed., *The Educated African,* pp. 519–532. New York: Praeger, 1962.

McCullough, Merran, Margaret Littlewood, and I[delette] Dugast. *Peoples of the Central Cameroons.* London: International African Institute, 1954. 174 pp. Describes the Bamun, Bamiléké, Tikar, and other Cameroon highland groups. The chapter on the Bamiléké is based on the excellent work of Delarozière and is the only full statement in English of the Bamiléké social system.

Meek, C. K. *Land Tenure and Land Administration in Nigeria and the Cameroons.* London: H. M. Stationery Office, 1957. 420 pp.

Mohammadou, Eldridge, *Histoire du Tibati.* Yaoundé: Editions CLE, 1968.

Mortimer, Edward. *France and the Africans, 1944–1960: A Political History.* London: Faber and Faber, 1969. 390 pp. See headnote.

Murdock, George Peter. *Africa: Its Peoples and Their Culture History.* New York: McGraw-Hill, 1959. 456 pp. Probably the best full-scale treatment of African ethnography. The many Cameroon ethnic groups can be seen within their wider ethnographic context.

Mveng, Englebert. *Histoire du Cameroun.* Paris: Présence Africaine, 1963. 533 pp. See headnote.

Mviena, P., and J. Criaud. *Géographie du Cameroun.* Yaoundé: Imprimerie de St. Paul, 1960. 111 pp. Designed for elementary schools, this little book provides a concise résumé of Cameroon geography.

Njoya, I. A., ed. *Histoires et coutumes des Bamoun.* Translated by Henry Martin. Mémoires de l'IFAN Centre du Cameroun: Populations, No. 5. Yaoundé: IFAN Centre du Cameroun, 1950. 232 pp. Njoya, Sultan of Bamun (1884–1933), created a unique alphabet in which his scribes wrote this history of the Bamun people.

Ritzenthaler, Robert and Pat. *Cameroons Village: An Ethnography of the Bafut.* Publications in Anthropology, No. 8. Milwaukee, Wis.: Milwaukee Public Museum, 1962. 147 pp. A well-done study, with illustrations, of Bafut society and of their chief, the Fon. The Fon discussed in this study is the same chief who is the hero of Gerald Durrell's delightful account of animal collecting in the Southern Cameroons, *The Bafut Beagles.*

Rudin, Harry R. *Germans in the Cameroons, 1884–1914.* New Haven: Yale University Press, 1938. 456 pp. See headnote.

Stanford Research Institute. *The Economic Potential of West Cameroon*. Menlo Park, Calif.: The Institute, 1965. A comprehensive survey of the economy of West Cameroon in eight volumes and several appendixes, prepared on contract for the West Cameroon government.

Stoecker, Helmuth, ed. *Kamerun unter deutscher Kolonialherrschaft*. Berlin (East): Rütten and Loening, 1960. 288 pp., fold-out map. Four studies, including one by Hans-Peter Jaeck ("The German Annexation"), two by Adolf Rueger ("The Revolt of the Policemen," "The Rise and Condition of the Working Class under the Cameroonian Colonial Regime"), and one by Hella Winkler ("The Cameroonian Proletariat, 1906–1914"). All four studies approach the subject from a Marxist-Lenininst perspective.

Tardits, Claude. *Les Bamiléké de l'Ouest Cameroun*. Paris: Berger-Levrault, 1960. 187 pp.

Vernon-Jackson, H. O. H. *Language, Schools and Government in Cameroon*. New York: Columbia University Teachers College Press, 1967.

Victoria Centenary Committee. *Victoria Southern Cameroons, 1858–1958*. Victoria: Basel Mission Book Depot, 1958. 103 pp. A short but well-conceived social, economic, and political history of the Southern Cameroons.

Warmington, W. Alan. *A West African Trade Union*. London: Oxford University Press for the Nigerian Institute of Social and Economic Research, 1960. 150 pp. Designed to complement the Ardener, Ardener, and Warmington volume (see above), this short work deals with the growth, activities, and structure of the Cameroons Development Corporation Workers' Union.

Welch, Claude E., Jr. "The 'Kamerun Idea' " and "Toward Federal Union in the Cameroons." In *Dream of Unity: Pan-Africanism and Political Unification in West Africa*, pp. 148–249. Ithaca: Cornell University Press, 1966. See headnote.

Articles

Alima, Jos-Blaise, and Jacques de Sugny. "Cameroun: Cent peuples, deux langues, une nation." *Jeune Afrique,* No. 457 (Oct. 1–7, 1969), pp. 58–68.

Ardener, Edwin. "Cautious Optimism in West Cameroon." *West Africa,* Sept. 30, 1961, p. 1071.

———. "The Kamerun Idea." *West Africa,* June 7, 1958, p. 533; *ibid.,* June 24, 1958, p. 559.

———. "The Political History of Cameroon." *World Today,* XVIII, No. 8 (Aug. 1962), 341–350.

"Assembly Charts Course for Cameroons." *United Nations Review,* April 1959, p. 15.

Brutsch, Jean-René. "Fernando Po et le Cameroun." *Etudes camerounaises,* No. 43–44 (March–June 1954), pp. 67–78.

"Cameroon Comes to Stay." *West Africa,* April 30, 1966, p. 479.

"Cameroon Complexities." *West Africa,* April 23, 1966, p. 447.

"Cameroon's Man in the Centre." *West Africa,* Feb. 24, 1968, pp. 211–212. Biographical vignette of Ahidjo.

"Cameroun." *Afrique,* No. 6 (quarterly supplement, 1966). Whole issue devoted to Cameroon.

"Cameroun: L'Eglise contre l'Etat?" *Jeune Afrique,* No. 508 (Sept. 29, 1970), pp. 32–35.

"Cameroun, dix ans d'indépendance." *Europe-France-Outremer,* XLV, No. 457 (Feb. 1968). Whole issue devoted to Cameroon.

"Le Cameroun dix-huit mois après l'indépendence." *Europe-France-Outremer,* XXXVIII, No. 379 (June 1961). Whole issue devoted to Cameroon.

"Cameroun, situation favorable," *Europe-France-Outremer,* XLVI, No. 474–475 (July–Aug. 1969). Double issue devoted to Cameroon.

"Cameroun, six ans de gouvernement Ahidjo." *Europe-France-*

Outremer, XLIII, No. 436 (May 1966). Whole issue devoted to Cameroon.

"Cameroun, trois ans de réunification." *Europe-France-Outremer,* XLI, No. 416 (Sept. 1964). Whole issue devoted to Cameroon.

Chaffard, George. "Cameroun à la veille de l'indépendance." *Europe-France-Outremer,* XXXVI, No. 355 (June 1959), 65–78.

Chilver, E. M., and P. Kaberry. "From Tribute to Tax in a Tikar Chiefdom." *Africa,* XXX, No. 1 (Jan. 1960), 1–19.

Clignet, Remi, and Frank Jordan. "Ecological Analysis as a Prerequisite to Social Planning." Unpub. monograph, Program of African Studies, Northwestern University, 1969.

"Compromise in Cameroon." *West Africa,* July 7, 1962, p. 742.

"Les condamnations de Yaoundé." *Jeune Afrique,* No. 524 (Jan. 19, 1971), pp. 28–31.

Decraene, Philippe. "Le Cameroun en quête de paix et d'unité." *Le Monde,* March 12 and 13, 1965.

Delarozière, R. "Cameroun: Inventaire ethnique et linguistique du Cameroun sous mandat français." *Journal de la Société des Africanistes,* IV, No. 2 (1934), 203–208.

de Schaetzen, Yves. "Cameroun 1970: Bilan et perspectives." *Marchés tropicaux et méditerranéens,* XXVI, No. 1263 (Jan. 24, 1970), 175–181.

Devernois, Guy. "Cameroons 1958–59, From Trusteeship to Independence." *Civilisations,* IX, No. 2 (1959), 229–234.

Ducat, Marc. "Cameroun, du mandat à l'indépendance." *Marchés tropicaux du monde,* Nov. 21, 1959, pp. 2547–2554.

Eyinga, Abel. "Opposition en démocratie." *Cahiers d'éducation civique* (Cercle Culturel Camerounais, Yaoundé), No. 4 (1963).

Gardinier, David E. "Reactions of the Douala People to Loss of Hegemony, 1944–1955." Ohio University Papers in International Studies, No. 3. Athens, O.: The University, 1966.

Gaudemet, Paul-Marie. "L'Autonomie camerounaise." *Revue*

française de science politique, VIII, No. 1 (March 1958), 42–72.

Gonidec, P. F. "Les institutions politiques de la République Fédérale du Cameroun." *Civilisations*, XI, No. 4 (1961), 370–395; XII, No. 1 (1962), 13–26.

Hodgkin, Thomas. "The French Cameroons," a series in *West Africa* beginning Dec. 18, 1954, and running through Jan. 8, 1955 (four issues).

Horner, George R. "Togo and the Cameroons." *Current History*, XXXIV, No. 198 (Feb. 1958), 84–90.

"Independence Foreshadowed for French Cameroons." *United Nations Review*, Dec. 1958, p. 30.

Johnson, W. R. "The UPC in Rebellion: The Integrative Backlash of Insurgency." Unpub. paper, 1967.

Kaberry, Phyllis M. "Traditional Politics in Nsaw." *Africa*, XXIX, No. 4 (Oct. 1959), 366–383.

Kingue, Michel Don, *et al.* "Cameroun, une entité aux visages multiples." *La Cité* (Paris), No. 21 (Dec. 1964), pp. 16–41.

Kitchen, Helen. "Cameroun Faces Troubled Future." *Africa Special Report*, III, No. 1 (Jan. 1960), 14–15.

"The Last Federation." *West Africa*, April 2, 1966, p. 371.

Le Vine, Victor T. "Calm before the Storm in Cameroun." *Africa Report*, VI No. 5 (May 1961), 3–4.

——."A Contribution to the Political History of Cameroon: The United Nations and the Politics of Decolonization—the Termination of the British Cameroons Trusteeship." *Abbia* (Yaoundé), No. 24 (Jan.–April 1970), 65–90.

——. "The Other Cameroons." *Africa Report*, VI, No. 2 (Feb. 1961), 5–6, 12.

——. "The Politics of Partition in Africa: The Cameroons and the Myth of Unification." *Journal of International Affairs*, XVIII, No. 2 (1964), pp. 198–210.

"Le Marché camerounais," special issue of *Marchés tropicaux et méditerranéens*, XX, No. 963 (April 25, 1964).

Migeod, Frederick. "The British Cameroons: Its Tribes and

Natural Features." *Journal of the African Society,* XXIII, No. 91 (April 1934), 176–187.

"Mission's Report on the Two Territories: End of Trusteeship Proposed for the French Cameroons." *United Nations Review,* March 1959, p. 31.

"Moskau's Taktik im schwarzen Erdteil." *Ostprobleme,* XII, No. 4 (Feb. 19, 1960), 112–115.

Strothmann, Dietrich. "Unter dem Diktat der Angst." *Die Zeit,* Mar. 8, 1969, p. 2.

Vandercook, John W. "The French Mandate of Cameroun." *National Geographic* LIX, No. 2 (Feb. 1931), 225–260.

Warmington, W. Alan. "Prospects for the Cameroun Federation." *West Africa,* Sept. 30, 1961, p. 1073.

———. "Savings and Indebtedness among Cameroons Plantation Workers." *Africa,* XXVIII, No. 4 (Oct. 1958), 329–343.

Welch, Claude E. "Cameroon since Reunification." *West Africa,* Oct. 19, 1963, p. 1175; Oct. 26, p. 1213; Nov. 2, 1241; Nov. 9, p. 1271.

Index

Abéga, Martin, 125
Action Paysanne, 69, 115
Afana, Osende, 128, 181
Agriculture, 36-38, 165-168, 183-184
Ahidjo, Ahmadou, vi, xix, 13, 25, 26, 55, 81, 82, 83, 85, 86, 94, 99, 103, 104-108, 110-112, 114, 128, 130, 131, 133, 135, 142, 143, 154, 155, 158, 165, 168, 179, 180, 181, 182, 183; government of, 20, 27, 55, 180; becomes Premier, 25; becomes federal President, 28; on "unified" party, 106-107; on ideology, 117; on civil servants, 142-143; on economic development, 161-162
Apple, R. W., 172n
Ardener, Edwin, 6n 43n, 46n, 94n, 95, 98
Ardener, Edwin and Shirley, 58, 59n
Assalé, Charles, 20, 106, 115, 118, 125, 134
Association Bantoue Efoula-Meyong, 15, 118-119
Aujoulat, Louis, 18
Azikiwe, Dr. Nnamdi, 22

Baeschlin-Raspail, Beat Christophe, 122n
Bakossi, 155-157; *see also* Tombel massacre
Bamiléké, xxi, 48, 51, 52, 53, 54-56, 68, 69, 127, 155, 184; *le problème Bamiléké*, 54-56, 157-158
Bassa, 47, 51

Bauxite, Martap deposits of, 34, 170
Berrill, Kenneth, 30n, 42, 56
Betayéné, Jean Faustin, 84
Beti-Fang, 47, 51, 53
Beybey Eyidi, Dr. Marcel, 104, 113; arrest and trial of, 108-109
Biafra, 175
Bilingualism, 73, 75
Bismarck, Prince Otto von, 4
Bloc Démocratique Camerounais (BDC), 18
Blum, Léon, 11
Bouchaud, Joseph, 2n
Britain, influence on Cameroon coast of, 3-4
Buell, Raymond Leslie, 10n

Cameroon Development Corporation (CDC), vi, 37-38, 160
Cameroon Development Corporation Workers' Union (CDCWU), 58
Cameroon National Union (CNU), 58, 99-102, 120, 136, 154, 161; founding of, 111-113; Congress of 1969, 132-134
Cameroon Outlook, 79
Cameroon Times, 79
Cameroon United Congress (CUC), 99, 112
Cameroons Champion, 78-79
Cameroons Federal Union (CFU), 22
Cameroons National Federation (CNF), 23

201